Children's Games
from Many Lands

Edited by

NINA MILLEN

FRIENDSHIP PRESS • NEW YORK

First printing 1943
Second printing 1944
Third printing 1945
Fourth printing 1946
Reset and redesigned 1951
Sixth printing 1953
Seventh printing 1956
Eighth printing 1958

Dedicated to

the Children I Know Best

My Nieces

J O A N   A N D   R U T H   P A I S L E Y

Acknowledgment

THE author wishes to acknowledge her indebtedness to Miss Anne Shannon of the Friendship Press, who has given enthusiastic help in the collecting of the material for the book.

Credit is due to the following individuals, boards, and publishers for permission to quote from their publications:

Board of National Missions of the Presbyterian Church in the U. S. A., for material in *Alaskan Play Hour,* by Katharine E. Gladfelter.

Board of Foreign Missions of the Presbyterian Church in the U. S. A., for material in "Rainbow Packet."

Home Mission Board, Southern Baptist Convention, for material in *Carmita of Cuba,* by Marjorie Jacob Caudill.

The Committee on Missionary Education and the Literature Department of the Woman's Missionary Society of the United Church of Canada, for material in *A Highway of Friendship,* by Isabel G. Uren.

Edinburgh House Press, for material in *Practical Books: India,* by Winifred Warr.

Board of Education of the Methodist Church, for material in *The Elementary Teacher.*

Marion Holcomb Skean, for material in *Circle Left.*

The Yale University Press, for material in *The Cheyenne Indians: Their History and Ways of Life,* by George B. Grinnell.

The American Antiquarian Society, for material in "Games of the Makah Indians," by George A. Dorsey, in Volume 23 of *The American Antiquarian,* 1901.

The American Anthropologist, for material in "Games of the Teton Dakota Children," by J. Owen Dorsey, in Volume 4 of *The American Anthropologist,* 1891.

Friendship Press, for material in *Africa: Loose Leaf Series; Chil-*

v

dren at Play in Many Lands, by Katharine Stanley Hall; *Filipino Playmates,* by Jean Moore Cavell; *Jewels the Giant Dropped,* by Edith Eberle and Grace W. McGavran; *New Joy,* by Carolyn T. Sewall and Charlotte Chambers Jones; *Rafael and Consuelo,* by Florence Crannell Means and Harriet L. Fullen; and *Welcome House,* by Jessie Eleanor Moore.

Acknowledgment is also made for material from "Games of the North American Indians," by Stewart Culin, in Volume 24, 1902-03; and "The Eskimo about Bering Strait," by Edward William Nelson, in Volume 18 of the Reports of the *Bureau of American Ethnology,* 1896, 1897.

Contents

GAMES OF AMERICA NORTH OF MEXICO   132

ALASKA   133

CANADA   136

UNITED STATES   147

GAMES FROM EUROPE   183

INDEX   211

Introduction

IF you could put on the magic "Seven League Boots" and travel from country to country, everywhere you would find children, and everywhere those children would be playing. Moreover, if you watched their games, you would find that many of them were basically familiar to you.

In spite of differences in names, words, and rules, the games children play follow a pattern that is similar. On your "Seven-League-Boot" visit you would watch the children of Africa playing "Killing the Elephant," Cuban children playing "The Fountain," the boys and girls of Peru playing "The King May Pass," and the children of Chile playing "The Hen Runs." After looking for a while, you would exclaim, "Why, it is *London Bridge!*" In Africa, in Asia, in Europe, and in the Americas you would see many varieties of "Fox and Geese," "Tag," "Hide and Seek," and "Blindman's Buff." You would come to the conclusion that not only is play universal among children, but that many of the games played are also universal. Games such as "Drop the Handkerchief" and "The Mulberry Bush" have been played and enjoyed for centuries.

The children in some countries play much more than in others, that is true. In some places children do not have time for play because they are set to work at an early age in order to aid their families. For example, the children of the Moslem countries and the Indian boys and girls of South America do not have many games. The desire to play is there, but they have no time for it because of the family duties that they must early assume.

The boys and girls of America can be shown how to put

on the "Seven League Boots" of imagination in order to see the children of other lands at their play They can be told what and how other boys and girls play. Better than that, they can actually play some of the games of other lands, as described in this book. Through such games they can discover a basis of understanding with children the world over.

There are many ways of using these games creatively. The more thought and care the leader puts into planning their use, the more the children will get from the play.

The simplest and most obvious use of the games will be to give enjoyment. New games are particularly stimulating. The enjoyment of a game brings with it many by-products of which the children realize little, but for which the leader may consciously plan. Playing a game teaches the children to know one another better, and it gives them practice in taking turns and being good sports. Playing a game relieves tension, releases pent-up energy, and so prepares the children to receive the other types of teaching that may follow.

In playing these games, the children will gain knowledge about the boys and girls of other lands. The rhythmic games of Africa and the singing games of Latin America and of India will tell the children something of the characteristics of the people of those countries. Games similar to "Fox and Geese" cannot help but teach the children something of the animal life of other lands, since this familiar game is played as "Eagle and Chickens" in China, as "Fox and Hen" in Turkey, as "The Hen and the Leopard" in Cameroun, Africa, as "The Street of the Tompeate" in Mexico, and as "The Coyote and the Father" among the Indians of this country. Games in which the children act out daily tasks, as in "The Mulberry Bush," will teach a little about the customs of other countries. The singing games will show what the music of other lands is like and the titles will teach a little about other languages.

During the study of any given country, the games of that

country may be played. The children may be led to seek knowledge of the country within the game itself. For example, during a study of Africa the children might play the Kikuyu game, "Our Work Is Done Like This." From it they will learn how wood is chopped, how fires are built, how water is carried, how corn is ground, and how babies are carried in Kenya. Other games will show what fruit trees and vegetables are common in the various countries.

The greatest values that will be gained are the unconscious ones. In playing the games the children will enter into a fellowship with other children the world over. They will see that boys and girls in Africa, Asia, and South America have just as much fun at games as they do. They will come to think of those children as potentially pleasant companions and of their countries as interesting places in which to live. Thus the basis of future friendly relationships will be laid.

The games may be played on playgrounds or in gymnasiums, in church school rooms during recreation periods, or at parties. If many are being used, it would be well to follow a few active games with some quiet ones.

Sometimes the leader may wish to use games as part of a story and play hour. Plans for such an hour might include a short introductory talk by the leader in which she describes the setting for the games to be played; the playing of a very active game, a less active game, and a quiet game in turn; the telling of a story by the leader. Stories from various countries, suitable for telling to children, may be found in Friendship Press books for children.

One of the essentials of a successful play period with children is enthusiasm on the part of the teacher. Such enthusiasm stems from an interest in the games themselves, an enjoyment in playing them, and a knowledge of why and how they appeal to children. The teacher needs to know the kind of games that will interest her group so that she may make a wise selection. A game that will please five-year-olds will not always appeal to eleven-year-olds, and lively boys will usually demand more active games than their quieter sisters. For the teacher's guidance, the age-group for which each game is intended has been noted in italic letters under the game title. The sex group is also indicated in those games that are played by girls or boys alone. Where the word "players" is used, the implication is that the game may be played by either boys or girls.

A short introductory note will be found preceding each section of the book. In these notes the chief characteristics of the games within the section are outlined. The leader will find such information useful when she comes to explain the games.

The games in this book have been collected over a period of more than two years. Hundreds of letters have been sent out to people who seemed to be likely sources of information regarding games played by children of many lands. Mission boards cooperated generously by sending the names of missionaries home on furlough. Contact was made with people of other nationalities living or visiting in this country. The result has been the collection of this series of representative games from many countries, including the main mission fields and a few of the little known ones as well. Wherever possible, the name of the individual or group contributing the game has been appended to the description. Games have been obtained from such out-of-the-way places as Kenya, Burma, Togoland, and New Guinea. In order to round out the collection, resort was made to authentic collected sources, in cases where game descriptions could not be obtained for certain countries or racial groups. The games in this book should prove comprehensive enough to enable the teacher to lead her pupils into a fellowship of play with children of many different lands.

Games from Africa

THE games included in this section are, for the most part, those played by Negro children in the villages of Africa. Because such children live in the open, their games are naturally played out of doors. Many of their games can be adapted for playing indoors, although a fairly large space will usually be necessary for them. The game descriptions indicate which ones may be adapted to indoor playing

As might be expected, there are a number of games that either imitate or are suggestive of hunting, since hunting still plays a part in the providing of food for the African Negro family. Games such as "Killing the Antelope," "Hunting the Leopard," and "Ebenga" are of this type.

The Negroes of Africa are very rhythmic. So we find that many of their games are accompanied by chanting or clapping or stamping or by all three. The players are sometimes more interested in the rhythm of a game than they are in competing to win it. Some of their games, such as the variety of "London Bridge" played in Cameroun, may seem long-drawn-out and uninteresting to children in this country. The leader should point out to them that the children of Africa take so much pleasure in the chanting of the repeated phrases and in the dramatic byplay that they do not pay much attention to winning the game. Indeed, the idea of winning a game in competition does not have so strong an appeal for them as it does for boys and girls in this country. To African children the playing of the game is likely to be more important than the winning of it.

Angola

WHAT IS BIG?
(Cinene Nye?)

10-40 players, all ages   *Indoors or out of doors*

People of the Ovimbundu tribe, unlike Americans, have a background of leisure. Play, however, is not confined to leisure hours. They possess the happy faculty of injecting an element of play into everything they touch or undertake. In their most sacred rites and ceremonials there are dances. Such dances are prominent features and closely connected with the planting and harvesting of crops. Each feast has its steps and drums and there can be no dancing without a song. Songs accompany their several labors. There is always a song leader and all the others sing the responses and chorus, accompanying the words with clapping of the hands and stamping of the feet. The following song about the elephant is one of the most interesting and it is one that is enjoyed by children and grown folks alike:

LEADER: *Cinene nye?*	What is big?
CHORUS: *Cinene onjamba.*	Elephant's big.
LEADER: *A cinene nye?*	Oh, what is big?
CHORUS: *Cinene onjamba.*	Elephant's big.
Kinyama viosi	Among the animals
Ka ku li ukuavo.	Of all the world
	There is no larger.

After this refrain the leader changes the song, indicating the change by chanting the word "Chameleon," meaning that he can change his song as the chameleon changes his color. The chorus respond by chanting "Crab," meaning that they can follow the leader, just as a crab can proceed in any direction.

LEADER:	*Elenalo!*	Chameleon!
	Malanga lomala vahe!	Cheetah and his children!
CHORUS:	*Hale!*	Crab!
LEADER:	*Ngeve lomala vahe!*	Hippopotamus and his children!
CHORUS:	*Hale!*	Crab!
LEADER:	*Hosi lomala vahe!*	Lion and his children!
CHORUS:	*Hale!*	Crab!
LEADER:	*Ngue lomala vahe!*	Leopard and his children!
CHORUS:	*Hale!*	Crab!
LEADER:	*Elenalo!*	Chameleon!
	A cinene nye? etc.	Oh, what is big? etc.

Leaders who wish to play this game with primary children may use the words of only the first part of the song, having the English words sung to a sort of chant accompanied by stamping and clapping. Junior children may wish to learn the whole song.—*From material prepared by Mrs. Bessie Cherry Fonvielle McDowell, Angola.*

NUMBERS

8-20 players   *Indoors or out of doors*

This is a game played by children of the Ovimbundu who are old enough to count. The group marches around the room or in a circle out of doors until the leader calls out a number in the Umbundu language. The players divide into groups according to the number called; that is, when the leader calls, "Three," the children divide into groups of three. They march until the leader calls another number, then change their grouping according to it. The Umbundu numbers are as follows: one, *mosi;* two, *vali;* three, *tatu;* four, *qualla;* five, *talu.* —*Mrs. Kathryn Avery Tucker, Angola.*

Cameroun

THE HEN AND THE LEOPARD
(Ngale Kup Ba Ze)

Indoors or out of doors   *Similar to Fox and Geese*
8-25 players, boys and girls, 6-12 years

Two children are selected to be the Mother Hen and the fierce Leopard. The other children are the Chickens. They form a long line behind the Mother Hen, each holding the next player around the waist. The Leopard stands in front of the line, swings in rhythmic movements, and growls. The Chickens all sway and chant as the Leopard growls.

The Mother Hen sings in a chanting voice, "The Leopard comes to catch you!" The Chickens chant in reply, "Poor children! Poor children!" With a particularly loud snarl, the Lepoard makes a grab at the Chickens, who all fall to the ground. If the Leopard catches a Chicken before it falls, it must leave the group and watch until all the others are caught.—*Mrs. Gayle C. Beanland, Yaounde, Cameroun.*

KILLING THE ANTELOPE
(Woe Nkok)

6-20 players, boys, 8-16 years   *Out of doors*

The players stand in two lines some three or four feet apart, facing each other, beside a place in the village street that is straight and smooth. Each boy is given a small, pointed stick. One of the fathers brings from the forest a large round fruit about the size of a coconut, maybe a breadfruit or a grapefruit. The father stands in the street and rolls the ball carefully and slowly between the lines of boys. As the ball passes them, the boys throw their sticks at it. The boy who first hits the moving ball wins the point. The ball or fruit is called an *nkok,* which is the native name for a small brown antelope. The boy who hits it is said to have "killed the antelope."

The game then starts all over again and goes on and on as other boys are given a chance to "kill the antelope."

With older boys, the fruit selected is smaller and the pointed stick is a spear with a sharp head. In this way the boys become expert in throwing the dart or spear at a moving object and they are trained for their future task of furnishing the family with fresh meat from the forest.

In playing the game in this country, a soft ball or basketball and blunt sticks rather than sharp ones might be used. The boy who manages to hit the ball with his stick could be said to have "killed the antelope." The game may be played either along a smooth piece of ground outdoors or on the floor of a room.—*Mrs. Gayle C. Beanland, Yaounde, Cameroun.*

CLAP-BALL
(Bivôe Ebuma)

10-30 players, boys and girls, 8-14 years   *Indoors or out of doors*

A line is drawn straight down the middle of the village street. The players line up in two equal rows facing each other, about six feet on either side of the dividing mark.

An orange, grapefruit, or a mock orange may be used for the ball. If the children are lucky, they may have an American rubber ball or baseball. Or they may have a ball made of crude rubber from the trees in their own back yards. One of the players is chosen to toss the first ball.

The ball is tossed back and forth across the line from one side to the other. Any player may catch it, but he *must not* step across the line. When the ball is caught, all the other players clap and stamp their feet just once. Should the ball not be caught by a player, the "tosser" takes it and throws it again. The ball should be kept moving very fast, for this game loses its interest if it lags.

This is a splendid group game, since all the players take part all the time with their clapping of hands and stamping of feet to denote that the ball has been caught.

In this country the game could be played over a line drawn on the ground or on the floor of a room.—*Mrs. Gayle C. Beanland, Yaounde, Cameroun.*

KILLING THE ELEPHANT
(On Njok)

Indoors or out of doors   *Similar to London Bridge*
                8-20 players, 6-12 years

One player is chosen to be the Mother and all the others, except two who form the arch, are the Children. The Mother with her Children passes under the arms of the other two. A Child is caught each time that the line passes under the arch. Each Child caught is drawn aside and asked to make a choice between such articles as a cake of gourd seed and a peanut porridge, a necklace of beads and a bow and arrow. According to their choice, the children are ranged in lines behind the two who make the arch until only one remains with the Mother. This one is now called the Only Child.

The game now takes on a particularly African flavor, with a chanted dialogue and many repeated phrases. The Mother and the Only Child retire to a distance or hide themselves. The Mother comes forth from time to time and tosses a handful of grass or waves her hand toward the others, who ask her in chorus, "How old is the Only Child now?"

MOTHER: The Only Child creeps.

CHORUS: *He e e!* How old is the Only Child now?

MOTHER: The Only Child walks.

CHORUS: *He e e!* How old is the Only Child now?

The dialogue proceeds as the Only Child grows up, is married, and has a baby. Then the Mother, now a Grandmother, is asked questions about the Child of the Only Child.

CHORUS: How old is the Child of the Only Child now?

MOTHER: The Child of the Only Child creeps.

CHORUS: How old is the Child of the Only Child now?

The Grandmother responds with one phrase after another explaining that "he walks, he sets traps, he has killed a little antelope, he has killed a big antelope," until at last "he has killed an elephant!"

"*He e e!*" shout the chorus as this climax is reached. The hidden player, who was the Only Child in the first part of the game, now comes forward and acts the part of the Child of the Only Child. One player after another comes to beg a piece of elephant meat from him. One after another is refused until a player comes forward who pleases him and to whom he gives an imaginary piece of the meat. The two run away together, all the others following.—*From "Children at Play in Many Lands," by Katharine Stanley Hall.*

Congo

ANTELOPE IN THE NET
(Kasha Mu Bukondi)

Indoors or out of doors   *Similar to Cat and Rat*
10-30 players, 6-10 years

One child is chosen to be It. The other children form a circle around him, holding each other's hands. "Antelope in the net" (*Kasha mu bukondi*), they chant over and over. It runs hard against their clasped hands and tries to break through in place after place. When he does, he runs away and the others chase him until he is caught.

Another child is then chosen to be It, probably the one who did the catching, and the game proceeds.—*Mrs. Esma R. Booth, Belgian Congo.*

THE CAT AND THE RAT
(Kameshi Ne Mpuku)

Indoors or out of doors   *Similar to Jungles*
20-30 players, boys and girls, 8-14 years

This game, played by the Luba tribe in the Southern Belgian Congo, begins by dividing the group into three or four equal lines, which stand parallel to each other. The players of each line hold hands, thus forming aisles between the lines. One player is chosen to be the Rat, and he runs around and through the aisles followed by another who is the Cat. One player standing in the lines is chosen to call for changes in position. When he shouts, *"Mpuki, ekale"* (meaning "Let the Rat stop," or literally, "That the Rat may stop"), the players drop each other's hands, take up a position at right angles to the one previously held, and join hands with the players who are now standing beside them. The aisles between the lines now run in a different direction. As the leader calls, the lines change direction quickly, hoping to confuse the runners until the Cat catches the Rat. The players must all turn in the same direction in changing positions. Then the runners reverse positions and the former Rat becomes the Cat and chases the other as Rat. When that Rat has been caught, two other players are chosen as runners. Or, if a certain Cat and Rat should run too long without any result, they may be changed by choosing other players.—*Mrs. Esma R. Booth, Belgian Congo.*

THE SNAKES
(Banyoka)

6-20 players, boys and girls, 6-8 years   *Out of doors*

This is a game played by the Bemba tribe of the Southern Congo and Northern Rhodesia. It is best played on thick grass.

The players divide into two or more groups, preferably with not fewer than six players and not more than twenty in each. The players then form themselves into a Snake by sitting on the ground one behind the other. Each player has his legs outspread and he encircles the body of the child in front. The different Snakes should be in parallel lines and moving in the same direction. The players then inch the whole line forward by waving their bodies back and forth to the tune of some lively song. Each line tries to go faster than the others, and the fastest one wins.

Variation: Snake of the Trails

Often this game is played by just one line with no purpose other than the enjoyment of the rhythm.

The boys form a long line, sitting on the ground, each one holding fast with his legs to the one in front of him. The line twists and curves around over the ground. The one in front chants as the players twist around, "Snake of the trails!"

The rest of the players chant this reply to the leader, "He's a twister, heigh oh, my boys, heigh oh!"

As the leader says his words and the others answer, he gives a sudden twist or two in one direction or the other. All the boys must follow him. The leader may curve so suddenly and quickly that sometimes the long Snake breaks in the middle. This causes great amusement.—*Newell S. Booth, Jr., Belgian Congo.*

ANTELOPE
(Mubwabwa)

Indoors or out of doors   *Similar to Tag*
10-20 players, boys and girls, 9-14 years

This is a game of the Luba Kasai tribe in the Belgian Congo. The *mubwabwa* is a small antelope that can run very fast. The game is played on a field somewhat the size of a tennis court with definite boundaries understood.

The game begins with the players choosing one of their number to be the *Mubwabwa*. He tries to catch the others. While doing so, he must from time to time yell out, *"Mubwabwa!"* The first player caught yells, *"Mubwabwa!"* and helps the original *Mubwabwa* to catch the others. The game continues in this way until everyone is caught, the last one being the winner. The players must stay within the boundaries of the field. If they get out at any time, they are counted as caught.—*Newell S. Booth, Jr., Belgian Congo.*

THE RAT IN HIS HOLE
(Mpuku Mu Kina Kyandji)

12-30 players, 8-14 years   *Indoors or out of doors*

This game comes from the Chokwe tribe in the Southern Belgian Congo. It can be played by either boys or girls, but not by a mixed group. It has many variations as to the names of the animals used; for instance, rabbit and fox, hare and dog. But the method of playing is similar in all the variations.

The game starts by choosing one player to be a Rat and another to be a Cat. The rest of the players form a ring facing inwards. They make the circle fairly tight by standing with their feet and elbows touching. The Rat goes into the center of the circle, which is called his Hole. Then the Cat tries to break into the circle by squeezing between the players, who resist him. If the Cat breaks in, the Rat runs out and is chased by the Cat, who is allowed to leave the Hole freely. When the Rat wishes to re-enter his Hole, the ring allows him to pass, but tries to stop the Cat from following. The interest of the game is in the venturesomeness of the Rat, who comes out of his Hole when he thinks the Cat is looking the other way. Also the Cat dares or invites the Rat to come out by appearing to pay no attention to him. The Cat may enter the Hole either between two players or between the legs of a player. Girls usually enter only between two players.

When the Cat succeeds in catching the Rat, he becomes the Rat and enters the Hole, while a new Cat is chosen from those in the ring.—*Mrs. Esma R. Booth, Belgian Congo.*

TA MBELE
(Pronounced, Tom Bailey)

Indoors or out of doors   *Similar to Simon Says*
12-30 players, 7-14 years

Usually the boys play by themselves and the girls by themselves. The players are lined up facing each other in two rows about four feet apart. The one who has been chosen to be It comes out into the middle and dances up and down between the line rows, while all the others clap their hands rhythmically and chant, *"Ta Mbele."* Suddenly It stops before a player and shoots out one of his hands. The one who is chosen has to throw out his hand at the same time. The point is that he has to match the leader's choice of right or left hand. If he does, he may be It. If not, the first It goes to somebody else.—*Mrs. Rhoda Armstrong, Kibonga Mission Station, Belgian Congo.*

East Africa

EBENGA

6-20 players, usually boys, 8-12 years   *Indoors or out of doors*

A cross section of bamboo root is cut into a disk, and the players take long spears of bamboo and line up in two lines, thirty to forty yards apart, facing each other. The first player in one line rolls the disk along the ground in front of the second line, pushing it with his spear. The players in that line throw their spears at the disk. Each hit means that the successful thrower takes a captive from the other side. The first player in the second line takes his turn with the disk and rolls it along the ground in front of the first line while the players throw at it. The game ends when all the players on one side have been taken captive. In this country a softball may be used in place of the disk and laths or slender sticks in place of bamboo spears.—*From "Africa: Loose Leaf Series."*

LIBA

Indoors or out of doors   *Similar to Jackstones*
4-10 players, usually girls, 8-12 years

This game is played with palm nuts. The players are seated in a circle on the ground around a large heap of palm nuts.

The first player throws one nut into the air and before it comes down, she swoops up with the right hand as many nuts as possible from the heap. The next player follows the same procedure. The one who picks up the largest number of nuts in an agreed number of throws wins.

A variation of this is played by making several little shallow holes in the sand and putting four to six nuts into all but one. The players sit about in a circle and one girl throws a nut into the air. Before it comes down, she picks up all but one nut from a hole and puts them into the empty one. If she is not quick enough to do this and catch the first nut before it falls, or if she leaves more than one nut in the hole, the next player takes her turn.—*From "Africa: Loose Leaf Series."*

HAND CLAPPING GAME

Indoors or out of doors   *Similar to Simon Says*
10-30 players, 8-14 years

The players form two parallel lines, facing each other. The first player in one of the lines becomes the leader. The leader and the player opposite him hold their arms up in the air. The leader quickly brings his down, clapping his hands together, and throws out one hand, left or right as he wishes. The one opposite must follow his movements simultaneously and throw out his hand to match the first. If he throws out the left and the leader the right, or vice versa, he is "wounded" and drops to the end of the line, the player next him taking his place. If he throws out the proper hand, then the leader is "wounded." Anyone "wounded" three times is "dead." When the leader of one side is "dead," his opponent becomes leader. The game continues until all but one are "dead." This game is played in various forms in many districts of Africa. —*From "Africa: Loose Leaf Series."*

Kenya

OUR WORK IS DONE LIKE THIS
(Mawira Maitu Ni Ogwo)

Indoors or out of doors　　　　*Similar to The Mulberry Bush*
6-20 players, girls, 8-12 years

The players divide into two groups. The groups form two lines and face each other, allowing a space of about ten feet between the lines. The girls of one side take two slow steps forward, as though to take possession of the stage. They begin to sing, "This is the way we chop our wood, here in the land of Kikuyu." As they sing, they make the rhythmic motions of the Kikuyu women cutting wood.

When they have finished singing, they take two steps backward into position in their line and the opposite group take two steps forward to take the stage. They sing, "We build our fire like this, here in the land of Kikuyu," stooping to lay dry wood on the coals of fire and kneeling low with their heads near the ground to blow it to a flame.

The first side again take the stage and sing as they perform, "We carry our water thus (in a gourd placed on our heads), here in the land of Kikuyu."

The game continues as they sing, "We oil our bodies thus, here in the land of Kikuyu" (rubbing the skin of their entire bodies with an imaginary mixture of castor oil and red clay). "We grind our corn thus, here in the land of Kikuyu" (kneeling to grind the soaked, cracked corn between two stones with the movement of a woman using a washboard).

"We carry the baby thus, here in the land of Kikuyu" (patting imaginary babies who are being carried on their backs in a sheepskin). As they slowly move their bodies from side to side with the movement of a cradle, they sing a Kikuyu lullaby. In this country the words may be sung to the tune of "Here We Go Round the Mulberry Bush." The words will fit if they are slightly changed to "This is the way we build our fire, etc."—*Mrs. Virginia Blakeslee, Kenya.*

HUNTING THE LEOPARD
(Gucaria Ngari)

6-20 players, boys, 10-14 years   *Out of doors*

This is a dramatic game and through it Kikuyu boys get practice in hunting. Each player is armed with a long stick, sharpened at one end to represent a spear, and a long bush-knife or a stick to represent one. A leader is chosen, and a playing ground where there is a clump of bushes is selected. The players discard any clothing they may be wearing from their waist up and line up in two rows facing one another. The leader chants a hunting song that goes something like this: "May the skin of the leopard that took four goats from the flock be punctured by the spears and arrows of these warriors. May his legs be broken, his eyeballs bruised, and his head become pulp. All hail to the warrior whose spear first enters his body."

The leader throws a green sprig between the two rows of boys, who then take up the same hunting song, thrusting their sharp sticks into the ground around the sprig as they sing. The two lines of boys now form two parties. One takes its position at the head of an imaginary ravine in which the leopard is supposed to be hiding. The second party forms a line extending across the imaginary ravine at a lower point. Cautiously the driving party pretends to beat down the brush with their bush-knives as they move forward in extended formation toward the company stationed below. The line of beaters moves gradually nearer the stationary line of boys.

Nothing but the one clump of bush jungle, a likely place for the hunted beast to take refuge, now lies between the two lines of boys. The clump is surrounded by the two lines. Each boy holds his sharp-pointed stick in readiness to strike in his left hand, and proceeds to beat down the remaining cover with the bush-knife held in his right hand, cautiously drawing nearer toward the center.

There is a succession of blood-curdling snarls made by the leader to imitate the snarl of a cornered leopard. The boys throw their sharp sticks with skill and force, which sends them ploughing into the earth several inches from the point where the imaginary leopard crouches, ready for a leap through their ranks.

The boys form a circle and dance around the space where their sticks have been thrust through their imaginary foe, singing a hunting song of victory, which they punctuate with wild shouts of rejoicing.—*Mrs. Virginia Blakeslee, Kenya.*

Liberia

JUMPING GAME

6-30 players, 6-12 years   *Indoors or out of doors*

The group stands in a circle, each clapping his or her hands and singing to a native rhythm song. Any rhythm song may be substituted by groups in this country, providing that it has speed and action. "Jingle Bells" would do very well, the music being sung without the words. Usually the players are all boys or all girls.

It stands in the center with hands on hips, hopping from one foot to the other and always extending the leg that is in the air so that the toe points downward. It advances to a child in the ring, hops and extends the right or left foot with toe pointed. The player in the ring must respond quickly by jumping and pointing the same toe as the leader. That is, if It extends her right leg and toe, the player in the ring must extend her right leg and toe. Thus the toes will not hit. If the player in the ring makes a mistake, the toes will hit, and the player must exchange places with It. If the player does not make a mistake, It must jump to another in the ring and try to catch her.—*Miss Ethel S. Emerick, Liberia, West Africa.*

CALL MY NAME

10-30 players, usually girls, 7-12 years   *Indoors or out of doors*

The children form a circle and choose one player to be It, who stands in the center. Those in the ring join hands and skip around in a circle singing "Call my name," and inserting the name of It in the song.

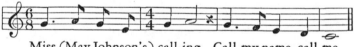

Miss (May Johnson's) call-ing   Call my name, call me.

It skips over to one of the players in the circle, touches her on the arm, and exchanges places. The group immediately changes the name in the chorus to that of the new It, who skips to the center of the circle and then out again to touch another player on the arm. The action is very lively and the changing of players is continuous. The game continues until all have had a turn at It or until they tire out. The Africans put a lot of rhythm and quick action into the game. Sometimes as they change places, they swing their arms, or beat time, snap their fingers, or clap their hands. Often the group drops hands and joins in the hand-clapping or snapping of fingers as they continue to dance around the circle.—*Miss Elsie Otto, Monrovia, Liberia, West Africa.*

Nigeria

ONIDE COMES
(Booko)

Indoors or out of doors   Similar to Hide the Thimble
5-20 players, boys and girls, 6-10 years

The leader holds a small stone in his hand. Another child runs and hides, and the remaining children sit on the ground and hold out both their hands. As the leader goes by them, he touches each hand with the stone. Secretly he places it in one hand. Meanwhile all the children sing:

> Onide comes,
> Saworo, Onide comes,
> All right! Onide,
> Come and inspect us.

When they come to the end of the song, the child who is hiding comes out and tries to find which player has the stone. He has three guesses. If he is successful in finding the stone, he takes his place with the group and the child who had the stone goes and hides. Then the game proceeds as before. If the player is not successful in three guesses, the group takes hold of him gently and ridicules him. If the player is a boy, then they put him on the ground. This child does not get angry, but laughs with the others. The Yoruba children are not easily offended and they enter heartily into the fun, even if the joke is on themselves.—*Mrs. George Green, Ogbomsho, Nigeria.*

HIDE OH! HIDE OH!
(Bojuboju)

Indoors or out of doors   *Similar to Hide and Seek*
6-20 players, 6-12 years

One player is chosen to be It. The others form a ring around him and the leader. The leader covers It's eyes closely with his hands. As he sings the following verse, the other players run and hide before the leader uncovers It's eyes: "Hide, hide oh! Richman is coming! Hide, hide oh!"

When the children have hidden, they call to the leader to open It's eyes: "Uncover them, uncover them!"

The leader sings, taking away his hands: "I will uncover them, I will uncover them!"

It then runs to find and catch the other players. He tries to tag each one before he or she can get back to the ring or base. Those who are caught help to catch those who have not been found.—*Mrs. George Green, Ogbomsho, Nigeria.*

WHO HAS FEATHERS?
(Kini o Ni Iye?)

4-20 players, 8-12 years   *Indoors or out of doors*

Each child holds a long leaf pulled from a tree. The leader stands facing the group and calls the name of things that do and do not have feathers. He asks, "Has a bird feathers?" to which the children should reply, *"Beni"* (Yes). He asks, "Has a house feathers?" to which the children should reply, *"Beko"* (No). If a child says, *"Beni,"* when he should have said, *"Beko"* (pronounced be-kaw), the others flog his legs with leaves.—*Mrs. George Green, Ogbomsho, Nigeria.*

PINCHING THE FOOT
(Jamolibanna)

3-10 players, usually girls, 5-7 years   *Indoors or out of doors*

One child is chosen to be It. The other players sit on the ground in a line with their feet stretched out in front of them. It stands facing them. Pointing at a foot she says:

Nini nini kills twenty,
Nini nini kills thirty,
Nini nini kills fifty.
One was a chief,
And one was a king—
Ogundele, the Blacksmith,
Take in your foot.

As she chants this verse, the one to whom she points takes in her foot. So the game proceeds, the leader repeating the above words over and over. On speaking the last line, the child at whose foot she points takes in her foot. The last remaining foot is pinched by the entire group as they chant the verse in chorus. Then the game is repeated, the child whose foot was pinched becoming the new It.—*Mrs. George Green, Ogbomsho, Nigeria.*

Sahara Region

TAIA-YA-TAIA

Indoors or out of doors   *Similar to Tag*
6-20 players, 6-10 years

The children of the Sahara region play "Taia-ya-taia" (pronounced tie-ah-yah-tie-ah). All the players but one stand in a row. One of the players who has been chosen It stands and faces them and shouts "Taia-ya-taia." Then he hops off on one foot as though lame. The other players run after him and touch him. He tries to catch one of those who touched him. If he can do so without putting down his foot, the person who is caught must be It for the next game.

South Africa

FEATHER GAME

4-12 players, 8-12 years   *Out of doors*

Kaffir children like to play a game with goose quills or long, heavy feathers. Each child takes seven feathers and puts them in a circle, tips toward the center. Then, at a signal from the one chosen as leader, each child picks up a quill from his circle and throws it at a tree that has been chosen. The child whose feather goes nearest the tree wins. The game proceeds until all seven feathers have been thrown.—*From "Lutheran Boys and Girls." Used by permission.*

Togoland and Gold Coast

THE HAWK
(Awako)

10-30 players, 5-10 years   *Out of doors*

This game and the three following are enjoyed by the children of the Ewe tribe of Togoland and the Gold Coast.

Two players are selected to be a Hawk and a Hen. All the others are little Chicks. A large, rectangular field is marked off into three sections, with the largest section in the middle. The Hen stands in the section at one end of the field, the Chicks at the other. The Hawk stands in the middle section on the edge of the field. The Hen then calls, "Little Chicks, come!" (*Kokloviwo miva*). The Chicks start running toward the Hen. At the same time the Hawk starts out to run across the center of the field, with outstretched arms (signifying his wings). He tries to catch as many of the Chicks as possible as they cross the center of the field. He is not allowed to leave the center or pursue the Chicks after they have once passed him. Those Chicks who have safely passed him run to the Hen, while those who have been caught have to leave the field. Then the Hen moves to the other side of the field and the game starts over again, until all the Chicks have been caught by the Hawk.

One variation is to allow the Chicks who have been caught to turn to Hawks and assist the Hawk in catching the rest of the Chicks next time they pass.—*Dr. Erich F. Voehringer, British Mandated Togoland.*

THE BIG SNAKE, or BOA CONSTRICTOR
(Da Ga)

Indoors or out of doors　　　　　　　　*Similar to Tag*
12-30 players, 8-14 years

A place, about ten feet square, is marked off as the Home of the Snake. One child is chosen to be the Snake and he retires to the Home, from which he then starts out to catch the other children. When he has caught one, the two must hold hands and go on catching in this way. Any further child that is caught must join the Snake by holding hands. Thus the Snake gradually grows in length. To be caught, a player must be touched by the free hand of the child on either end of the Snake.

Whenever the Snake breaks because the children in the Snake have let go their hands, then the free children may touch the Snake and thereby force it to return to its Home. The Snake breaks up and its members run to the Home as fast as they can, being thrashed lightly by the free children until they reach safety. In the Home the Snake reassembles and starts out again to catch the others. The game ends when all children are caught and have been embodied in the Snake. The one caught last is the winner.

A favorite trick of the Snake, when it is long enough, is to try and encircle the other children and thus catch them. In that case the free children may try to break the Snake by force and thus cause it to run to its Home, if they can do so before being touched by either the head or the tail. The one who started the Snake is the captain and may decide how the Snake should be assembled; that is, who should be at either end and who should be caught next. It is well to mark the boundaries of the field, to avoid endless running around.— *Dr. Erich F. Voehringer, British Mandated Togoland.*

MAKING SLAVES
(Kluviwowo)

Indoors or out of doors   *Similar to Prisoners' Base*
10-30 players, 8-14 years

Two lines are marked off on the ground from forty to sixty feet apart. The players are divided into two groups, which stand opposite each other along the lines. The first player of Team I starts off to win a slave. He walks toward the players of the other team, who await him along their line, standing with right hands outstretched. He slaps three hands in succession, either at random or three times on the same hand. When he has slapped the third hand, he starts running back to his own side while the owner of this hand pursues him to catch him. If he reaches safety behind his own line before being caught, his pursuer becomes his slave and has to take his stand behind his master. If he is caught before reaching the line, he becomes slave to the pursuer and has to return with him to the other side and stand behind his master. Then the first player of Team II walks over to get a slave from Team I (or to be made one, if he is caught). The second player of Team I then has a turn, and so on down the line. If a player who already owns some slaves himself is made slave to another, all his slaves, too, become the property of the new master and have to line up behind him. Once a player becomes a slave he can take no more active part in the game, but must stand behind his master. The game ends when one player has become master of all the others.—*Dr. Erich F. Voehringer, British Mandated Togoland.*

THE TWO FRIENDS
(Kholo Eveawo)

9-25 players, 8-12 years   *Indoors or out of doors*

The children line up in pairs and one child who is It stands at the head of the file. It calls, "I am seeking a friend" (*Mele kholo dim*), and claps his hands. At this sign the last two children start running forward, one on either side of the file, past It, who then runs after them to catch one before the two meet each other. If the two friends succeed in meeting, *i.e.,* if they are able to join hands before either is caught, they take their places at the head of the line. Then It has to return to his place in front of them and call for the next couple. If It succeeds in catching one of the two before they join, the one caught becomes his friend. The two of them take their places as the first couple of the line. The remaining player becomes It and starts calling and trying to catch a new friend. The game goes on until each couple has had one run. (The two friends who are on the run must meet in front of the group.) —*Dr. Erich F. Voehringer, British Mandated Togoland.*

Games from Asia and the Pacific Islands

THE games played by children in Asia and the Pacific Islands are extremely varied in character, as might be expected from the immense area of the continent and its outlying islands and from the wide differences in the racial groups represented. We find that the children of China play games that show imagination and speak of a deep culture. We discover that children in Iran play games that mirror a nomadic type of life. We notice that boys and girls of New Guinea enjoy a dramatic game that pictures the simple hunting life of their people and their close contact with the animals of the jungle. Everywhere we find that the children's games reflect something of the life of the people, whether they have been enjoyed for centuries or recently introduced and adapted.

Among the games from the great continent of Asia we find some whose pattern is already familiar to us. "Hide and Seek" and "Tag" are everywhere. Variations of "Fox and Geese" appear in many countries. In Burma and in the jungles of New Guinea, a type of "Button, Button" is played. "Stone, Scissors, Paper," a counting out game, is played not only in all parts of China, but in Japan, Korea, and Indonesia as well, which probably indicates a common origin. Japan shows an imaginative and interesting variation of the game in "The Old Woman, the Lion, and the Warrior." A rather rough game of India, played with two sticks, is enjoyed also by the boys of Iran and China (but probably not by their mothers). Characteristically, the girls of India play singing games, accompanied by rhythmic clapping of their hands.

Children of other countries will have fun learning these interesting games from Asia. As a beginning, try "Water Sprite" from China, "Water Pots" from India, and "Nose, Nose, Nose, Mouth" from Japan.

ASIA

Arabia

AIRPLANE
(Thiara)

Out of doors   *Similar to Tag*
4-30 players, boys and girls, 6-12 years

The game is played near trees or on the playground where there are swings, seesaws, and steps on which the players can stand.

One player is chosen to be It and he represents an airplane. It tries to tag his fellow-players while they are running from place to place. No player can be tagged as long as he is off the ground; that is, when he is standing on the root of a tree or in its branches or when he is on the seesaw, steps, or swings. When a player is tagged, he becomes the next It. —*R. G. van Peursem.*

MARBLES
(Theelat)

Out of doors   *Similar to Marbles*
2-4 players, usually boys, 8-12 years

Three holes, each about the size of a fist, are dug about five feet apart in a piece of level ground. Each player has one marble and plays for himself.

The first player shoots his marble from a line drawn some twenty feet away from the first hole. The players shoot in turn, one after another. The player who gets his marble into a hole or hits the marble of another player gets another turn.

The marbles are shot into the first hole, then into the second and the third. A turn is made and the marbles are shot back to the second and the first holes. Another turn is made and this is kept up until the "tenth hole" is reached. The player who first gets his marble into the tenth hole wins the game.—*R. G. van Peursem.*

Burma

ROCKING

6-15 players, 5-7 years   *Indoors or out of doors*

The children sit in a line one behind the other on the floor or ground, with their feet stretched out straight in front of them, touching the back of the one ahead. They stretch out their hands to reach the shoulders of the child ahead, and in that position they sing to a tune of their own. Children in this country may use the tune of the chorus of "Jingle Bells" instead.

> All together, all together,
> Now we rock and rock,
> Just like birdies in the trees,
> Sing and rock and rock.
>
> All together, all together,
> Oh, what fun for all!
> Just like birdies in the trees,
> Look out! Whee-ee-ee! We'll fall!

As they sing, "We'll fall," the children all tumble over.
—*Mrs. Gordon Gates, Burma.*

HIDING STONES

Indoors or out of doors   *Similar to Button, Button*
8-30 players, 6-10 years

The children are divided into two sides, each with a leader. They are seated in parallel lines on the floor or ground, with the feet out straight ahead and close together, touching the back of the player just ahead. The leader or a player chosen by him is to hide a small stone under the knees of a child on his side. The chosen one goes up and down the line, putting his hand under the knees of each child in the line, as if to drop the stone there. He finally leaves the stone under one pair of knees, as carefully as possible so as not to attract attention, being sure to put his hand under the knees of the other children in the line, after the stone has been placed. The leader of the other line then tries to guess where the stone is. If he guesses correctly, a child from the other side must join his side, and he now has the privilege of hiding the stone. If he guesses incorrectly, a child from his side must go over to the other side, which again has the chance to hide the stone. Each line tries to increase its number. The side with the largest number wins the game.—*Mrs. Gordon Gates, Burma.*

HOP SCOTCH

Usually out of doors   *Similar to Hop Scotch*
2-10 players, 7-10 years

"Hop Scotch" is played by children of Burma in the same way as in America, except that the Burmese children squat on their heels with their hands on their hips, and when going from one-square to another, give a sort of jump over the lines without losing the squatting position.—*Mrs. Esther Josif, Rangoon, Burma.*

JUMPING-SEED GAME
(Khone-nyin-toe)

Indoors or out of doors   *Similar to Marbles*
2-9 players, all ages

This game is played in all parts of Burma. It is something like "Marbles"; but instead of marbles, the seeds from the long pod of a huge creeper are used. These seeds are like large beans, about an inch in diameter. In America, lima beans might be used in playing the game. Usually the number playing does not exceed eight or nine. There are no sides; everyone plays for himself.

Each player sets up a certain number of his seeds, anywhere between five and ten, in a long row. The seeds are placed on end on the ground, with the flat side facing forward, about an inch apart. The object of each player is to knock down as many as possible. This is done in the following way: The player kneels some five or six yards away, facing the row of seeds. He places the index finger of his left hand near the ground parallel to the row of seeds, with the back of the finger towards himself, and puts a seed in front of the finger at about the second joint. Then with the thumb and forefinger of the right hand he draws back the end of his left forefinger and suddenly lets go. The left forefinger thus strikes the seed squarely, shooting it towards the row of standing seeds. Considerable skill is required to keep the seed from jumping up and missing altogether. A particularly clever player is often able to "put a curve" on his seed and thus knock down a number of seeds at a time.

The most common way of playing is for each player to take all the seeds he knocks down, in one or three shots, but this is sometimes varied by having the player who knocks down the most seeds take all of them for himself.—*Miss Lucy F. Wiatt, Burma.*

HIDE AND SEEK

Out of doors   *Similar to Hide and Seek*
4-20 players, both boys and girls

The game is played by the Palaung children of Burma.

THE COUNTING OUT. First, a counting out game is used to decide who shall be It. Sometimes the children stand in a circle around a large stone or a tall stump on which each child places the first finger of one hand. The finger of each child must touch the fingers of the children on either side. One of the children repeats a familiar counting out rhyme and at each word or group of syllables touches a finger, one after the other. The child whose finger is touched on the last syllable of the rhyme becomes It.

Sometimes the children stand around a sapling for their counting out. They place their hands around it, one above the other. The one who is counting out touches their hands as the words of the rhyme are spoken. Sometimes the children do not hold anything, but place their closed fists one above the other, one hand only being used. When the first word of the rhyme is spoken, the child whose fist is at the bottom withdraws it and puts it on top. The second child follows suit with the second word and so on. The one whose hand is left at the bottom of the pile at the end of the rhyme is It.

THE GAME. It closes his eyes while the others hide. When they are all hidden, they call, *"Ku-ri,"* and then It starts hunting them. The hunting goes on until all are caught. The hidden players may call, *"Ku-ri,"* from time to time. The first to be caught becomes the next It.—*Mrs. Esther Josif, Rangoon, Burma.*

ROUND BASKET
(Chin-Lone)

Out of doors   *Similar to Football*
Any number of players, usually boys or men

The game of "Chin-Lone" is sometimes called "Burmese Football," though actually the only thing it has in common with football is that it is played with a kind of ball. In fact, it hardly seems like a game at all, for there are no teams and no points are scored. It is played with a light, hollow ball about four inches in diameter, made of strips of rattan carefully interwoven in bands so as to leave twelve pentagonal holes.

The players stand in a circle, and any number may take part. One player starts the ball, tossing it into the air with any part of his body except the hand, arm, or toes. The ball may be struck with the knee, the shoulder, the head, the heel, the bottom or the side of the foot, etc. Each player keeps the ball going as long as he can, either until he gets tired or until he makes an awkward stroke, sending the ball away from himself toward someone else, who then goes on in the same way. The game continues as long as anyone wishes to play. Players can drop out or new ones join in, of course, at any time.

"Chin-Lone" is really the national game of Burma and is played by both men and boys in all parts of the country. Though there is no competition for points, there is some competitive spirit in the effort to develop a high degree of skill. "Chin-Lone" is an excellent means of developing muscular coordination. In playing the game in America, a volleyball or lightweight, hollow rubber ball might be used.—*Miss Lucy F. Wiatt, Burma.*

China

CATCHING THE DRAGON'S TAIL
(Chuo Tung Wei)

10-30 players, boys and girls, 8-12 years   Indoors or out of doors

"I want to be the head," "I want to be the tail," the children are shouting as they make themselves into a Dragon. A Dragon is a line of boys and girls, each with his hands on the shoulders of the one in front of him. The first in the row is the Dragon's head. See it puffing fire? The last in the row is the Dragon's tail, eager to lash to the right and left and escape the head. But until the signal "Go!" is given, the Dragon must be a straight line. Someone counts, *"Em* (one), *er* (two), *san* (three), *ko* (go)."

On the signal "Go!" the head runs around toward the tail and tries to catch it. The whole body must move with the head and remain unbroken. The minute that anyone lets go of the shoulders in front of him, he breaks the Dragon's body and the Dragon dies. A new Dragon must be formed. If the head player touches the tail, he may continue to be the head. If the body breaks before he catches the tail, the head becomes the tail, and the next in line is the head, and so on until each has had a turn to be a fiery head and a lashing tail.

This game is also called "Eating the Fish's Tail."—*Mrs. Gertrude Rinden, Fukien, China.*

SEEKING FOR GOLD

Out of doors   *Similar to Marbles*
2-6 players, usually girls, 8-12 years

The game is played on the ground with a handful of pebbles, the prettier the better. It is more fun to play with a small group so that all may have a chance to play before the pebbles are taken.

The players sit in a circle on the ground. The first player drops the handful of pebbles to the earth. She draws a line with her finger between two of the pebbles and then tries to shoot one of them against the other. If the two pebbles click together, she takes both and has another turn. The player draws a line between two other pebbles and shoots again. If the pebbles click together, she gets them both and another turn. When she misses, the next player picks up the pebbles, drops them, draws her line, and proceeds to snap one stone against the other. The player who has the most pebbles after the game is over is the winner of the game.

SHUTTLECOCK
(Ch'ieh Tze)

One or more players, any age   *Indoors or out of doors*

If you can play "Mumblety-peg" with your hands, you may wish to try "Shuttlecock" with your feet. Buy or make a shuttlecock or use a badminton birdie. Chinese boys make shuttlecocks by cutting two feathers right straight down through the quills and putting these four feathers through a hole in a cash (a Chinese coin with a square hole in the center). The quills of the feather are braided for an inch on the under side of the cash, and bound tightly at the end.

Above the cash, the feathers flare out in four directions for two and a half inches above the coin. A shuttlecock must be light, and it must bounce well.

The player kicks the shuttlecock into the air with his foot and tries to keep it there with successive kicks. He counts and the game is to see how many times he can kick it up in the air before it falls to the ground. A beginner kicks it twice and it falls. An expert can kick it two hundred times! He looks as though he were doing a dance in the air with the white, feathery shuttlecock flying around him.

As in "Mumblety-peg," good players do more and more difficult things. The best players make rules about the order of the kicks and the part of the foot used. While the beginner keeps the shuttlecock in the air any way he can and kicks with any part of the foot, the advanced player follows this order: right toe, left toe, right outside of foot, left inside of foot, right inside of foot, left outside of foot, right heel, left heel, and so on. Try it!—*Mrs. Gertrude Rinden, Fukien, China.*

STRIKE THE STICK
(Da Tiao)

2-20 players, 8-12 years   *Out of doors*

Chinese boys and girls often play "Strike the Stick" because it requires so little equipment. It is a good game for school recess because it can be started and stopped in a hurry. Whenever the players have two sticks and two stones, "Strike the Stick" can be played. The first player lays a ten-inch stick across two stones. With another stick, which he holds in his hand, he flips the first stick into the air. If anyone in the group catches it in the air, he wins the next turn. If no one catches it and it falls to the ground, the player measures the number of stick lengths from the stones to the spot where the stick fell and that is his first score. The stick is still his.

His next play is to prop it against the stone so that one end is on the ground, and the other end is in the air. This time he strikes the end of the stick in the air, making it fly upward. Again each one in the group tries to catch it in the air so that he may have the next turn. If it falls to the ground uncaught, the player again measures the number of stick lengths from the stones to the spot, and adds this number to his score.

His third play is more difficult. He lays the stick across the stones again as in the first play and with the stick that he holds in his hand he flips it into the air. While it is in the air, he must bat it with the other stick. If he is successful in this play, he may bat it a long way off and thus his score will mount up very high. Three successful plays of this kind are enough for anyone, so the sticks are passed to number two in the group and so on. Anyone who catches the stick in the air may take his turn immediately. Otherwise a player keeps it through the three plays and then passes both sticks to the next in the group.—*Mrs. Gertrude Rinden, Fukien, China.*

TIGER TRAP

Indoors or out of doors   *Similar to Cat and Rat*
10-30 players, 6-10 years

Two players are chosen to be the Tiger and the Lamb. The other boys and girls take hands and stand in two lines about four feet apart, facing each other. The Lamb stands in the open space at one end, facing the Tiger, who stands at the open space at the other end. The Lamb calls, "Ba-a-a, ba-a-a!" and the Tiger dashes between the lines toward him. The players take hold of hands and close up the space at both ends of the rows, but the Tiger may manage to get down the line and catch the Lamb before the circle closes about him. The players try to keep the Tiger from catching the Lamb, who is running around the outside of the circle, bleating as he goes. If the Tiger does not succeed in breaking through to catch the Lamb before he has run around the circle five times, he must take his place among the other players, while the Lamb chooses a new Tiger. If the Tiger does catch the Lamb, he becomes the next Lamb and chooses a new Tiger to catch him. In that case, the Lamb joins one of the two lines and the game begins again.—*From "Children at Play in Many Lands," by Katharine Stanley Hall.*

STONE, SCISSORS, PAPER
(Ching, Chang, Pok)

2-40 players, any age   *Indoors or out of doors*

This is a game used in counting out or choosing It or deciding which team shall have first choice at play. The game can be played by either two individuals or by two teams. The object is the same in either case—to win the play over the opponent. In the play three signs are made: Stone, by forming the right hand into a fist; Paper, by holding out all the fingers of the right hand, palm down; Scissors, by holding out the first two fingers, with the thumb pressing on the last two fingers. Each one of these signs has a value with regard to the other two. Stone wins over Scissors because it can break them; Paper wins over Stone because it can cover it; Scissors win over Paper because they can cut paper.

In playing the game, the right hand is doubled into a fist. It moves up and down to each of the three signal words, *"Ching, Chang, Pok,"* spoken together by the players. On the third word, *"Pok,"* the players form the object they wish to represent. The winning player is the one who has made the sign that wins over the sign of the other player.

When two teams are playing against each other, a captain is chosen for each. The captain decides what sign shall be made and whispers his choice to the teammate next to him, who in turn passes it to the one next him, and so on down the line. The counting of the three words begins and on the word *"Pok"* each team makes the sign agreed upon. If both make the same sign, there must be another turn. The team with the winning sign has first choice.—*Edward Tong, Fresno, California.*

EAGLE AND CHICKENS
(Lao Yin Chuo Siao Chi)

Out of doors   *Similar to Fox and Geese*
                        8-20 players, 6-10 years

In Fukien Province there are eagles and hawks, which often swoop down from the mountains and carry off the chickens. The children have made a game about it. Even very small children like to play Eagle and Chickens, and they work very hard to keep out of the clutches of the Eagle. A line of boys and girls forms and each puts his hands on the shoulders of the one in front of him. The head of the line is the Mother Hen and all the others are Chickens. The player at the end of the line is the Chicken that the Eagle wants. The Eagle stands facing the Mother Hen five feet away. When the signal is given, the Eagle swoops down, running this way and that way, trying to clutch the end Chicken. Mother Hen and all the Chickens in between do their best to protect the baby Chicken at the end of the line. They must not let go of the shoulders in front of them.

They swing this way and that way to ward off the old Eagle. If the end Chicken is caught, he drops out of the game. The game may go on until all the Chickens are caught. All like to take turns being Eagle, Mother Hen, and baby Chicken on the end.—*Mrs. Gertrude Rinden, Fukien, China.*

HOP SCOTCH
(T'ao Fang Tze)

Out of doors   *Similar to Hop Scotch*
4 or 5 players

In Fukien Province there is a favorite kind of "Hop Scotch." It is played in a rectangle, which boys and girls mark off on the ground with a stick or sharp stone. They also divide the rectangle into eight or ten smaller rectangles. The first player throws a stone into space one, hops in, picks it up, throws it out, and hops out. If he does this without touching a line with his foot or stone, he continues to play. He throws his stone into space two, hops into one, and continues to hop on that same foot into space two, picks up his stone, throws it out, hops out. He goes on in this way into spaces three, four, etc. The upper left corner space is called "Public House." Here a player may always stop, put both feet down and rest. After one has gone completely through all the spaces without fault, he may choose any space and mark off a part of it for his private house where he may always rest on two feet, and where no one else may hop or throw a stone. He may not take one entire space, but only a portion of it, leaving a part or a pathway beside it for his fellow-players to hop into as they pass his house. Each player tries to win just as many private houses as possible.—*Mrs. Gertrude Rinden, Fukien, China.*

THE WALL OF CHINA

Indoors or out of doors   *Similar to Pom, Pom, Pullaway*
8-30 players, boys and girls, 8-12 years

A space about ten feet wide is marked off to represent the Wall by drawing two parallel lines straight across the center of the room or field. The player who is It takes his place in this space to defend the Wall. All the other players are Besiegers. At a distance of from fifteen to thirty feet from each side of the wall, other parallel lines are drawn. These mark the safety zones or home goals where the Besiegers stand. At a signal or cry of "Start" or "Ready" from the Defender on the Wall, all the Besiegers must cross the Wall to the goal on the other side. The Defender tags as many as he can touch without stepping out of the boundaries of the Wall. All who are tagged by the Defender must join him in trying to tag the rest of the players during future raids. The game ends when all have been caught, the last player taken becoming the Defender for the next game.—*From "New Joy," by Carolyn T. Sewall and Charlotte Chambers Jones.*

CALL THE CHICKENS HOME

Indoors or out of doors   *Similar to Blindman's Buff*
5-20 players, boys and girls, 6-9 years

One player is blindfolded and becomes the Blindman. The remaining players are Chickens. The Blindman says, "Tsoo, tsoo! Come and seek your mother." Then the Chickens run up and try to touch him without being caught. The one who is caught becomes the next Blindman and the game goes on.—*From "Children at Play in Many Lands," by Katharine Stanley Hall.*

WATER SPRITE

Out of doors   *Similar to Pom, Pom, Pullaway*
8-30 players, boys and girls, 6-9 years

There is an old Chinese superstition that after the rainy season, sprites or spirits live in the middle of the rivers and streams, and people passing along the banks might be lured by them into the water. The game of "Water Sprite" grew out of that tradition.

One of the group is chosen to be the Water Sprite. The remaining players are divided into two equal groups. Each group forms a straight line facing the other with a wide space between them. This space represents the river. The Water Sprite stands in the middle of the river and motions one of the players on one side. That player in turn motions to one of the players on the opposite side. These two players try to exchange places by running through the river. The Water Sprite tries to tag one of them before he reaches the opposite river bank. If he fails, he tries again. If he succeeds, that player becomes the Water Sprite.

India: Central

DEER AND LEOPARD
(Cheetal, Cheetah)

6-30 players, 8-12 years   *Out of doors*

The Cheetal (chee-tul) is the beautiful spotted deer that is found widely in India. The Cheetah (chee-tah) is the hunting leopard that is trained by Indian princes to hunt deer and antelope.

The players are divided into two equal sides and one person is chosen to direct the game. The. leader gives the name of Cheetal to one side and Cheetah to the other. Parallel lines are drawn about six feet apart. Along these lines the players stand, backs to each other, the Cheetals on one and the Cheetahs on the other. Two other parallel lines are drawn to form the home base for each side. Each is placed from fifteen to twenty feet behind the line along which the players of its side stand.

The leader takes his place between the lines of players at one end. He calls out "Chee-ee-ee-ee," and then suddenly ends up with either "tal" or "tah." If he says "tal," the Cheetals must race for their home base and the Cheetahs must turn and chase them. If he ends the word with "tah," the Cheetahs must turn and run while the Cheetals chase. Anyone caught before reaching his home base is out of the game, which goes on until all but one or two of the players have been captured.

It adds to the interest of the game if another pair of lines is drawn a yard or so behind the front line, with the ruling that anyone who dashes across this line before his side is called will be counted as caught and out of the game.—*T. N. Hill, Jubbulpore, India.*

TAG
(Kho)

Indoors or out of doors   *Similar to Tag*
10-30 players, 8-12 years

In this variety of tag game, the players squat about two feet apart along a line that has been drawn on the ground or floor. Alternate players face in opposite directions. The player who is It is free to cross and recross the line at either end whenever he wishes to do so, but he cannot cross through the middle part of the line. One of the squatting players is selected to give first chase to It and the game begins. This Chaser may not cross the line at all. He must stay upon the side that he was facing as he squatted in the line. If It crosses the line, the Chaser taps the back of any player facing the side to which It has crossed. The player thus tapped becomes the Chaser. He jumps up and tries to catch It, while the one who tapped him takes his place in the line. When It again crosses the line to the other side, the second Chaser taps someone facing that side, and a third Chaser takes up the hunt. This goes on until It is caught by another player, who then becomes the new It, while the former It becomes the first one to chase him.

Much skill is displayed by the Indian boys in tagging a player at the proper instant to enable him to get the advantage in the race.—*T. N. Hill, Jubbulpore, India.*

CIRCLE TAG
(Kho)

Indoors or out of doors　　　　　　　　　　*Similar to Tag*
8-30 players, 10-12 years

A player is chosen to be It and another to be the Chaser. The others stand in a circle each about two feet apart, with every alternate player facing inwards and the others facing outwards. The Chaser stands within the circle and It may be either within or without, at a safe distance from the Chaser. The game begins with the Chaser running after It, who must keep near the circle. He continually darts in and out of the circle in his desire to escape. Whenever It enters or leaves the circle, the Chaser must tag someone facing in the direction in which It is fleeing. This person now becomes the Chaser until It crosses the circle line in the opposite direction, when he must tag someone facing in that direction to take up the chase. When It has been caught, he becomes the Chaser and the one who caught him is It.—*T. N. Hill, Jubbulpore, India.*

India: North

LITTLE STICK, BIG STICK
(Guli Danda)

10-30 players, boys, any age   *Out of doors*

This game is played all over India by boys of any age. The equipment needed is a little stick, or *guli*, about six inches long and an inch and a half thick, sharpened at both ends; and a strong sturdy stick or *danda*, about two feet long and an inch or more thick.

A small hole is dug in the ground, big enough to put the end of the *danda* under the *guli*, which is laid across the hole. The hole should be about four inches wide and three inches deep.

Two captains are selected and they choose sides. The choice of who shall play first may be decided by a toss, much like "heads or tails." A stone that has been wet on one side is tossed into the air. The captains choose "wet" or "dry" sides, and the one who has guessed correctly the side that falls uppermost wins first play.

The first player takes the *danda*, holding it by one end like a baseball bat, using it as the occasion demands. He inserts the end of the *danda* under the *guli*, which he then flips upward with a quick movement, trying to fling it as far away as he can. Next, he goes over to the place where the *guli* has landed, and with his *danda* hits one of the pointed ends, thus flipping it up into the air. While it is still up in the air, he bats it with the *danda*, trying to knock it as far as possible from his original starting place, the hole. He has three turns to do this. If he misses the first, he still has two turns left; but if he hits it the first time, he has two chances to hit it again and get it still farther from the hole.

When his three chances are over, he returns to the hole and lays the *danda* beside it.

A player from the other side goes over to the *guli,* picks it up, and throws it at the *danda* on the ground. If he hits it, he takes his turn. If he misses, a player from the opposing team takes it.

There is no formal scoring for sides. The game may end at any time, or when all the players have had a turn.—*Miss Margaret Newton, Ludhiana, India.*

HIDE AND SEEK
(Mito Mitar)

Out of doors   *Similar to Hide and Seek*
                    6-20 players, 6-12 years

One player is chosen to be It, and the group selects a place as a goal to which It must go while the others are hiding. A home base is also chosen. It goes to the specified place and returns to the base without looking around, while the other players hide themselves. It begins to seek the others. If he finds one, he tries to touch him before the player is able to run and touch the base.

If any player has a chance to get back to the base, he may try it, but if he is touched on the way by It, he becomes the new It.

When one player has been touched and caught, the Seeker calls out his name so that all may hear that a new player is It.

The game begins anew. The new It goes to the appointed place and back to the base, while the rest hide as before.—*J. S. Robson*.

LALAMLALI

6-20 players, boys any age   *Out of doors*

Good sturdy sticks called *dandas* and a ball made of rags or rubber or an old tennis ball are needed for this game. Each *danda* should be about two feet long and an inch or so in thickness. Each player has his own *danda*. A fairly large playground is needed.

One player is chosen to be It. The other players spread themselves out over the playground from three to five yards apart. Each bends over and draws a circle around himself with the end of his *danda*. No player can go out of his circle during the game, unless he becomes It.

One of the players in the circle throws the ball as far away from all of them as he can. The one who is It must pick it up from where it has landed and throw it back to the players, trying to hit one of them or to have the ball stop rolling in his circle. If either thing is accomplished, that person changes places with It, surrendering his *danda* to him and becoming the next It.

The players in the circles are allowed to dodge the ball or bat it with their *dandas* if it comes near them, but they may not touch it with their hands.

If the ball does not make anyone It the first time, the one who is already It may throw the ball again from the place where it has stopped. Since this is probably much closer to the other players, he will likely secure a hit.

The game ends when the players want to stop.—*Miss Margaret Newton, Ludhiana, India*.

THE LION AND THE GOAT
(Sher Aur Bakri)

Indoors or out of doors   *Similar to Cat and Rat*
10-20 players, 6-8 years

One player is chosen to be the Lion and one to be the Goat. The other players form a circle, holding hands. The Goat stands within and the Lion without the circle. The Lion tries to touch the Goat with his hand, and the players in the circle try to protect the Goat. The Lion may break through into the circle and the Goat may then go outside the circle. The players in the circle let the Goat pass freely, but they try to prevent the Lion by moving their arms up and down. If the Goat is touched, he becomes the Lion, and the Lion chooses another player to become the Goat.—*J. S. Robson.*

India: South

WATER POTS

Out of doors   *Similar to Tag*
10-30 players, usually girls, 8-12 years

The group is divided into two equal sides. One group are the Water Pots, the other group the Runners. One of the Runners is It and must tag those running. The Water Pots squat in a line at about three- or four-foot intervals. The one who is It tries to touch one of those who are running back and forth between the Water Pots. Runners can dodge back and forth between the Water Pots, but It cannot. It must run down and around the end, trying to touch one. When It is tired of chasing, or wants to get a girl out, she suddenly squats beside a Water Pot and that Pot becomes It. This makes it easier to tag a girl and eventually as each It starts off a new tagger, all will have had a turn at being tagged. The sides then change and Runners become Water Pots.—*Miss Grace Bullard, Nellore, South India.*

WHO IS IT?

Indoors or out of doors   *Similar to Blindman's Buff*
8-30 players, usually girls, 6-10 years

The players form a circle. One is chosen to be It and she is blindfolded. She takes her place in the middle of the circle. One child from the circle is sent away out of sight. The other children dance around in a ring, singing the following verse:

One of us has gone a - way,
Who it is, you now must say;
If mis - take you do not make,
We'll clap our hands.—

At the end of the song, the blindfold is removed and It must look around and quickly guess which player has left. If she guesses wrong, she must be blindfolded and try again.

If she guesses right, she takes her place in the ring while the other players clap until the hidden one returns to the circle and becomes the next It.—*From "Practical Books: India."*

STICK DANCE
(Kolattam)

Even number of girls, 8-14 years   *Out of doors*

In the evening when the sun has lost a little of its burning heat, the schoolgirls of India like to gather under the shade of trees and dance. Their dances are very graceful and pleasing, and as they dance, they sing and keep time by clapping or by tapping sticks.

For this game, there must be an even number of girls. Each must have a pair of brightly painted sticks, which are made as gay as possible. Each line of the song may be sung twice over before going on to the next line.

At the beginning of the game the girls take partners and form a circle. The partners face each other, thus making an inner and outer circle. The girls in the inner circle kneel down on the left knee.

Throughout the dance the standing girls keep step with the song. The step, which should be lightly done, is one tapping step on the spot with the left foot alternating with one tapping step with the right foot, beginning with the left foot. On the first bar of each line the partners strike each other's sticks. They tap their right-hand sticks on one line, their left-hand sticks on the next, and both sticks at the beginning of each line of the refrain.

When the second line of the first verse is begun, the girls in the standing circle move to the left, each taking the next kneeling girl as her partner and tapping sticks with her. In this way, the standing girls move on to a new partner for each line of the song and refrain, until they arrive again at their original partners. At this time the inner circle stands and the outer circle kneels and the whole is repeated again.

Come maid-ens fair, al-to-geth-er come.

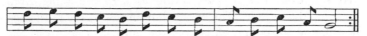

Danc-ing in a ring-o, round and round and round we go.

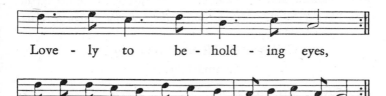

Love - ly to be - hold - ing eyes,

Danc-ing light-ly, clap-ping gai-ly, joy-ful-ly we sing.

Reverence to elders we must show.
Best of daughters we will always be.
  Lovely to, etc.
Lightly we step with tinkling bangled feet,
Holding rainbow-colored sticks in either jeweled hand.
  Lovely to, etc.
Now here's the end. Our song and dance are done.
We've tried with care to please you all and everyone.
  Lovely to, etc.

     —From "Practical Books: India."

NEEDLES FOR SALE

Indoors or out of doors   *Similar to Fox and Geese*
10-20 players, usually girls, 6-10 years

One player imitates a woman peddler, crying, "Needles, needles, needles for sale!" and walking as if she had a basket on her head All the other girls stand in a long line, holding each other by the waist. The one at the end says, "I'll buy your needles." At this remark, the Needle Seller makes a dash and tries to touch the end girl. The whole line must keep together and run from side to side, trying to keep the Seller from touching the end girl. The first girl in line especially must keep heading off the Seller. Of course, the purpose is not to let the line break. If it separates, then the girl who made the break must take the Seller's place. Or if the end girl is touched, she becomes the Seller.—*Miss Grace Bullard, Nellore, South India.*

CHRYSANTHEMUM FLOWER
(Chamati Puvvu)

6-20 players, girls, 6-10 years   *Indoors or out of doors*

The children form a circle, standing close enough to reach one another's hands easily. The girl who is It turns to her neighbor on one side. She claps her own hands together, beginning to sing a song about the chrysanthemum flower as she does so. She claps the left hand of her neighbor with her own right hand, then the right hand of her neighbor with her own left hand, then both hands of her neighbor's hands and then claps her own hands together again. After doing this with the neighbor on one side, she turns to the neighbor on the other side and repeats. Meanwhile all the other children clap their hands in rhythm. When playing the game in this country, the tune of "Jingle Bells" might be hummed in time with the clapping.—*Miss Emilie Weiskotten, Rajahmundry, India.*

GORA

12-30 players, boys and girls, 8-12 years   Indoors or out of doors

The players are divided into two teams each with a captain. The playing field is marked off, or boundaries are set for it, so that there is a goal line at one end. The teams decide which one shall have first turn and which shall have second. The team with second turn scatters over the field, between the center and the goal line. The team that has first turn forms into a line in the center of the field. The players stand close together, side by side, with their arms firmly linked. With the captain as a pivot, the line begins to revolve, like the spoke of a wheel, chanting, *"Go-ra, Go-ra!"* Suddenly the captain shouts, "Go!" (*Joa*), and immediately the line breaks. Each member of the line tries to reach the far side of the field without being caught by the players of the other team. Those who are tagged must fall out of the game and watch. The remaining players of the first team form another line and rotate as before. This goes on until all of the first team have been caught. Then the second team takes its turn in the center of the field, while the first team tries to catch it.—*From "Practical Books: India."*

Iran

SLAVES

10-20 players, usually boys, 8-12 years   Out of doors

The players are divided into two sides. Parallel goal lines are drawn about thirty feet apart, and another line is drawn midway between the two rows. One boy advances across the middle line toward his opponent's goal line. He tries to touch one of the players on the other side and run back again to his own side before he himself is tagged. As soon as a boy on the opposite side is tagged, he chases the one hitting him who runs toward the middle line. If the first player is tagged before he crosses the middle line, he is taken as a slave back to the opponent's side; if he gets over safely, another boy on his side dashes out and tries to tag the pursuer before he gets back to his base line. If he succeeds, he wins a slave. Each side has a prison where it keeps its slaves. As soon as one side wins, the boys get on the backs of the defeated and ride them back and forth several times.—*From "Children at Play in Many Lands," by Katharine Stanley Hall.*

KNUCKLE BONES
(Ashukh)

4-8 players, boys   *Out of doors*

Out in the ancient Bible land of Persia, which is today known as Iran, one may see a group of boys gathered around a large ring, playing a game that resembles "Marbles"; but instead of marbles, they use the knuckle bones of sheep, called *ashukh* (ow-shoock). These small bones are twirled between the thumb and finger and then shot at other bones placed in the center of the ring. The object is to knock the bones out of the ring and to leave the "shooter" within the ring and near the ones to be knocked out if the player is clever. Some of the bones will be colored in bright hues of blue or red; the fathers of certain boys may have been engaged in dying yarn for the famous rugs they make in Iran and the boy could slip in a number of bones and have them come out in beautiful colors. The boys become quite expert at the game and can shoot these small bones with a good deal of force and knock the others out of the ring—which is sometimes made as large as fifteen feet across.—*J. Christy Wilson, Tabriz, Iran.*

EAR AND NOSE
(Goosh va Damagh)

Boys and girls, 8-12 years   *Indoors*

The players sit in a circle. One is chosen as the Chief, who directs the play. Before the game starts, the players repeat together a rhyme, whose words are simply a jingle:

> *Ala hop, sang torop,*
> *Peshgel boz, khoda biamorz, hop!*

No one must laugh or smile or make any loud cries during the speaking of the rhyme or the playing of the game that follows. The Chief lightly pulls the ear or nose or hair of the player on his left, who then passes on the same action to the neighbor on his left. So the action passes around the circle until it reaches the Chief again. The Chief then starts another action around the circle, perhaps tickling or poking. Sometimes the action is funny and the children want to laugh. Whoever laughs or giggles or makes any noise has to leave the game. The winner is the one who shows the most control by not being put out of the game.—*Seyedeh Motamedi, Teheran, Iran.*

TAP, TAP, PASTE
(Tap, Tap, Khamir)

Boys and girls, 5-10 years   *Indoors*

One of the players is chosen to be It. He lies flat on the floor, face downward, with eyes hidden. The rest of the players gently tap him on the back, saying these words:

Tap, Tap, Paste!	*Tap, Tap, Khamir!*
Bottle full of cheese	*Shishe por paneer*
Whose hand is up?	*Dast kee balast?*

One of the players puts up his hand, then It must guess

whose hand is up. If he guesses correctly, he gets up. If he does not guess correctly, the other players tell him a story in rhyme:

> We went to the butcher store
> And bees on the meat there we saw.
> Do you know what they were saying?
> Zeelees, Weelees, Zeelees, Weelees.

The children make sounds like bees on the last line of the rhyme. Then they tickle It for a while. He then rises and the child whose hand was up becomes the next It.—*Seyedeh Motamedi, Teheran, Iran.*

WHO WAS IT?
(Kee Bood?)

8-20 players, 6-8 years   *Indoors or out of doors*

One of the children is chosen to be the Cat and the others are the Mice. The Mice stand side by side in a line. The Cat sits down at a short distance from the line, hangs her head, and closes her eyes. A fairly large-sized stone is placed between the Cat and the line of Mice. The Mice have a little stone.

While the Cat's eyes are closed, one of the Mice runs out from the line, taps the big stone with the little stone, while the other Mice sing:

> Little Mouse, little Mouse,
> Beware, the Cat may get you.

The Mouse runs back to the line while the children sing:

Who was it, who was it?	*Kee bood, kee bood?*
It wasn't I.	*Man na boodan.*

The Cat must guess the name of the child who stepped out and tapped the stone. If he guesses correctly, the Mouse takes the place of the Cat. If not, the Cat must guess again. —*From "Welcome House," by Jessie Eleanor Moore.*

WOLF AND FLOCK
(Gorgam va Gale Mibaram)

Out of doors   *Similar to Fox and Geese*
6-25 players, boys and girls, 8-12 years

One player is chosen to be a Wolf and another to be the
Shepherd. All the rest of the players are Sheep. They stand
behind one another in a line back of the Shepherd, each
holding on to the next player. The Wolf stands in front of the
flock of Sheep and the following conversation takes place:

WOLF: I am the Wolf and I have come to take away the flock.
SHEPHERD: The flock has a Shepherd and you can't.
WOLF: I will take away the best ones.
SHEPHERD: I won't let you have even the worst ones.

The Wolf then tries to catch a Sheep while the Shepherd
blocks him. The Sheep move behind the Shepherd in a line.
The Wolf sometimes breaks through and catches any Sheep
that he is able to touch along the line. The game proceeds
either until all but one of the Sheep are caught, that one being
considered the winner, or for a definite length of time, when
either the Wolf or the Shepherd is declared the winner, according to which has the most Sheep.—*Seyedeh Motamedi,
Teheran, Iran.*

PUCK AND HANDLE
(Pil Dasteh)

12-20 players, usually boys, 10-14 years   *Out of doors*

Away over in Iran in the country of Cyrus and Darius and
Xerxes, the boys, and sometimes the girls, play a game called
"Pil Dasteh." The first word is pronounced like our word
"peel"; the *a* of the second word is short. The *pil* or puck is a

stick a few inches long and an inch or so thick, and sharpened at each end. This is the "ball," if we should liken the game to "Rounders" or "One o' Cat." The other instrument is the bat or *dasteh,* which in Iranian means handle. The short stick is hit on either end. A sharp crack will send it spinning up into the air. Then the object is to hit it just as far as possible with the bat before it falls to the ground again. Should another player catch it on the fly, he comes to bat; otherwise, the first to get hands on the puck is allowed to throw it back at the bat, which lies on the ground. If he can hit the bat, it is his turn to take a round at knocking out the short stick. If he misses, the first player has another turn.

Parents sometimes object to the game because the short stick, being sharp on either end, may make a cut and is especially dangerous if anyone should be hit on the face or around the eyes. A dozen or more can play "Pil Dasteh," several being at bat and the others in the field. Some boys of Iran consider it even more fun because there is a bit of danger connected with it.—*J. Christy Wilson, Tabriz, Iran.*

Iraq

THERE WAS A MAN WHO HAD SIX GIRLS
(Rajul Uindhu Sitt Banat)

Indoors or out of doors   *Similar to The Mulberry Bush*
10-20 players, usually girls, 6-10 years

This singing and motion game is played by girls of all ages in northern Iraq, but it is probably common to all Arabic-speaking countries. The music is that of "Here We Go Round the Mulberry Bush," and the game is greatly similar. During the first part of the song the girls move in a circle, holding hands.

As each daughter is described, appropriate motions are made. The song:

> There was a man who had six girls,
> Had six girls, had six girls.
> There was a man who had six girls,
> And that is how it was.
> One of them was a washwoman,
> A washwoman, a washwoman.
> One of them was a washwoman,
> And that is how it was.

The rest of the girls may be baker, dressmaker, dancer (in making motions descriptive of an Arab dancer, the left hand should be on the hip, the right hand held above the head and fingers snapped while the feet stamp in rhythm), cook, schoolteacher, (here the girls usually stick out their chins and make ugly faces and the game ends in hilarity).—*Mrs. Helen G. Glessner, Kirkuk, Iraq.*

Japan

BIG LANTERN, LITTLE LANTERN
(O-ki cho-chin, chi-chai, cho-chin)

Indoors or out of doors   *Similar to Simon Says*
6-20 players, 6-12 years

The children sit in a circle on the floor or on the ground. The one who has been chosen It starts saying to the neighbor either on his right or his left, "Big lantern" (*O-ki cho-chin*). At the same time he makes the form of a large lantern with his hands. The person addressed then turns to either his right- or left-hand neighbor and says, "Little lantern" (*Chi-chai, cho-chin*), making with his hands the form of a little lantern. The play goes to whomever it is addressed, the new player turning to one on either side, thus keeping everyone in suspense as to where it is going next. The size of the lantern described with the hands and the words used must correspond; if not, the one missing is put out. At first, it is well to go slowly and all in one direction until the idea is "over" and a certain rhythm set. Then the speed can be increased and the directions varied. The Japanese generally get into such gales of laughter that they fail to enforce the rule of "putting out."—*Miss Katherine Fanning, Tottori, Japan.*

CAT AND MICE
(Neko to Nezumi)

Kindergarten children, any number   *Indoors*

This is a very popular game with kindergarten children in Japan. It has words to it which are sung; but before the game is half over, the excitement is at such pitch that no one thinks of the words, so I believe it might be played without them. The children make a circle, sitting in their chairs or on the floor. One child is chosen to be the Cat, and he may choose from the circle as many Mice as he has endurance to catch. The song tells the story of a family of mice who have found some food in the kitchen and are eating it. While they are eating, they crawl around on their hands and knees, within the confines of the kindergarten circle. The next verse of the song tells of their having finished their meal. They lie down to sleep in the kitchen. This the Mice do by snuggling all together in the middle of the floor.

Meanwhile the Cat has been in hiding behind the chair of one of the children and the third verse of the song tells of the large Cat who is on his way to the kitchen, and the children can see him as he slowly creeps in on his hands and knees. As he actually enters the circle, he meows a very large meow (which is what the Japanese say) and then the scramble is on. The Mice disperse, always on hands and knees and always in the circle, the Cat in exciting pursuit. As each Mouse is caught, he returns to his chair and the last Mouse caught has the right to choose another game. He will invariably choose this one if he has any strength left. It takes speed and endurance both for Cat and Mice; and knees get pretty sore as the Cat pursues and corners and the Mice dodge and duck.

Since all the players crawl on the floor, this game is always played indoors.—*Mrs. Ursul Moran, Osaka, Japan.*

THE DEVIL AND THE FROG
(Oni to Kaeru)

Indoors or out of doors   *Similar to Tag*
6-20 players, 6-10 years

With a stick, draw on the ground (or on the floor with chalk) the outline of a large lake with a very irregular coast line. Make many peninsulas and necks of land connecting bodies of water. The more irregular the coast line, the better.

One of the players is chosen to be the Devil and he must stay on the outside of the line that represents the lake. All the rest of the children jump into the lake and are Frogs.

The Devil cannot jump into the lake, and the Frogs cannot jump out. But the Devil runs around the lake, out onto the peninsulas and over the connecting necks of land, trying to tag from the shore one of the Frogs running around in the lake. Swiftness and a method of stampeding the Frogs sooner or later brings the Devil close enough to tag one. After a Frog is tagged, he has to get out of the lake. The last one tagged has the privilege of being the next Devil.—*Mrs. Ursul Moran, Osaka, Japan.*

CLAP
(Aan, Pon)

Indoors or out of doors   *Similar to Simon Says*
8-30 players, 8-12 years

With all the players sitting in a circle, the leader turns to a neighbor on either the right- or the left-hand side and says, *"Aan,"* putting the palm of his right hand under his chin, the fingers pointing to the person he addresses. That person continues by saying, *"Pon,"* putting his hand on his head, fingers pointing to the person he is addressing on either side of him. That person then turns to a neighbor on either the right or the left side, but instead of saying anything, he is mum and claps his hands. This order of action—that is, palm under chin, hand on head, and clap—must be maintained, but the direction of "passing on" is up to the choice of each individual. The point is to say the proper thing with the proper action, most difficult of all being not to speak when you clap. Those making mistakes should drop out of the game.—*Miss Katherine Fanning, Tottori, Japan.*

PORTRAIT PAINTER

10-30 players, 6-10 years   *Indoors*

Three to five children are chosen to be the Artists and they stand or sit before the rest of the group. They have large white papers tied over their faces, completely covering them. With brushes (camel's-hair brushes, such as those used in Japanese writing, are the best) dipped into ink, they simultaneously paint their own faces on the paper following the directions of the leader who gives some such orders as, "Draw the left eyebrow, the nose, the right ear, etc.," until the features of the face have all been named. The paper must be stiff enough to stay flat over the faces and to prevent the pressure of the brush from being felt, and a most humorous result is shown. Then the Artists are paraded about before they are given the privilege of seeing their own faces.—*Miss Katherine Fanning, Tottori, Japan.*

NOSE, NOSE, NOSE, MOUTH
(Hana, Hana, Hana, Kuchi)

6-20 players, 6-9 years   *Indoors or out of doors*

The players sit in a circle. The one who is It taps his nose and says, *"Hana, hana, hana,"* while all the other players imitate. On the next word, *"Kuchi,"* which means mouth, It taps his ear or some other feature. The players must touch their mouths when the word *"Kuchi"* is spoken. The names of the other features are *mimi* (ear), *me* (eye). The game should be played rapidly. If a player makes a mistake, he becomes the next It.—*From "Children at Play in Many Lands," by Katharine Stanley Hall.*

A COUNTING OUT GAME
(Jan, Ken, Po)

2-40 players, any age   *Indoors or out of doors*

This is a counting out game used all over Japan, even by adults, to decide who is It or to choose sides; or sometimes it is used as a "peacemaker" as well. In any argument or quarrel, the decision of *"Jan, Ken, Po"* is accepted without question, whether child or ricksha-puller be in the argument. Two players or three or a whole group may take part.

The two players stand opposite each other and extend their right hands with the fist closed. As they say together the words *"Jan"* and *"Ken,"* they pump their hands up and down, generally marking time with their feet as well. At the word *"Po,"* each forms his hand in one of three positions. He can leave it as it is, a closed fist, to represent a Stone. He can open it out flat to represent Paper. Or he can extend the first two fingers to represent Scissors. Each sign has a definite value with relation to the other two. Stone dulls Scissors, so Stone wins over Scissors. Scissors cut Paper, so Scissors win over Paper. Paper wraps Stone, and Paper wins over Stone.

If both players make the same sign, it is a tie and the process must be repeated until one wins over the other.

When three people are playing, the stronger sign wins even though there are two of the weaker; that is, one Scissors would be stronger than two Paper signs. If all signs are different, it is a tie and should be done over.

When two sides are playing, the leaders of each side make the signs to see which shall have first turn.

"Jan, Ken, Po" may also be played as a game, the purpose being to eliminate all but the final winner. The group divides into couples, each of which repeats, *"Jan, Ken, Po,"* and makes the signs.

The winner of each couple then turns to the winner of another couple and the process is repeated. Again the winners play against each other until eventually all are eliminated but one. He is declared victor and the others raise their arms above their heads and shout, *"Banzai!"* (Hurrah!).—*Miss Katherine Fanning, Tottori, Japan, and Mrs. Ursul Moran, Osaka, Japan.*

Variation:

A RELAY RACE

Two sides of equal numbers are chosen and seated in two rows facing each other. Each side selects a leader who mentally chooses which article (Stone, Paper, or Scissors) his side will represent. All players place hands behind backs and at a given signal the leader of each side, by placing his hands in those of a person next him, conveys which article he has chosen. This person in turn and in the same manner tells the one next him, and so on down the line. This must be done entirely by feeling and without looking. When all have been told, the two sides say, *"Jan, Ken, Po,"* in the usual manner. That side wins whose captain has chosen the winning article. Anyone on either side making a mistake must go over to the opposite side. The object is to see which side wins oftenest and gains the greatest number of members in a given time.—*Miss Eleanor E. Jost, Shizuoka, Japan.*

THE OLD WOMAN, THE LION, AND THE WARRIOR
(Obaasan, Shishi, to Samurai)

12 players, 8-12 years   *Indoors*

The necessary equipment consists of a screen projecting from the center of the wall at one end of the room, completely hiding two players from each other, while still leaving them both visible to the remaining players at the other end of the room. If the screen is not available, a blanket hung on a string may be substituted. A sheet is too thin, as the opponents' shadows are visible.

The players are divided into two groups of equal numbers. A leader is chosen from each team and each stands behind one side of the screen and a few paces back. The other players arrange themselves in rows in the other half of the room, ready for action when their turn comes. At a given signal, the two leaders step forward and meet at the edge of the screen, each representing either an Old Woman, a Lion, or a Warrior, according to his choice. The Old Woman walks feebly, bending over an imaginary cane; the Lion comes on all fours and may roar as he meets his opponent; the Warrior marches like a soldier, with right hand on imaginary sword at his left side.

Each player may either win or lose, according to the choice he has made, as the Lion overcomes the helpless Old Woman, the Warrior slays the Lion, and the venerable Old Woman is given first place by the Warrior. If the players happen to choose alike, they must repeat until one wins.

The winner now plays with the next player on the loser's side. That side loses whose final member loses to any member of the opponent's side.

The fun of the game comes in having all nonperforming players placed where they can see what each of the participants is about to represent.—*Miss Eleanor E. Jost, Shizuoka, Japan.*

OLD MAN AND OLD WOMAN
(Ojiisan, Obaasan)

Indoors or out of doors   *Similar to Jacob and Rachel*
10-20 players, boys and girls, 6-9 years

The players are seated in a large circle and one boy and one girl are chosen to represent an Old Man and an Old Woman respectively. The object of the game is for one to catch the other when both are blindfolded.

The two chosen are blindfolded with clean towels or large handkerchiefs, and the Old Man is given a small bell. Then each is led inside the circle and turned around several times, after which the Old Woman calls, "Grandpa," and the Old Man responds by ringing the bell. With outstretched arms, the Old Woman walks in the direction from which the bell sounds, trying to catch the Old Man while he tries to avoid her. At frequent intervals she calls, "Grandpa," to which he must always respond by ringing the bell. When he is caught, she receives the bell. Both players are turned around several times and the Old Man tries to catch the Old Woman in the same manner, calling frequently, "Grandma," to which she must always answer by ringing the bell.

When she has been caught, the blindfolds are removed and each bows to a successor, the Old Man choosing a boy and the Old Woman a girl. The game now proceeds as before.

Care must be taken that there is nothing inside the circle over which players could trip. If a bell or similar article is not available, when the Old Woman calls, "Grandpa," the Old Man may respond by answering, "Grandma," and vice versa.— *Miss Eleanor E. Jost, Shizuoka, Japan.*

SQUIRRELS WANT A HOLE

5-50 players, 6-8 years   *Similar to Pussy Wants a Corner*

This is played in two different ways, either with music or by counting, "One, two, three." In either case, the basis is the same. Several groups of three children are chosen to be Trees, and they stay in different parts of the room. Then as many children as there are Trees are chosen, and one extra. These are the Squirrels. Each one chooses a tree to stand beside. The extra one stands in the center of the room and counts, "One, two, three." On "three," the Squirrels beside the Trees run out and go to some other Tree, while the one in the center tries to get to a Tree. No Squirrel can be at the same Tree twice in succession.

If music is used, the Squirrels "play" around, picking up nuts or burying them to music; but at a thunderous clap of discordant chords from the piano, all scramble for the protection of a Tree. This is repeated for as long a time as it proves interesting.—*Mrs. Ursul Moran, Osaka, Japan.*

Korea

MEK KONK

5-20 players, 8-12 years   *Indoors or out of doors*

The players form in a line and each player has with him an equal number of pine nuts (any small nuts or stones will do). The player at the head of the line is the first to be It. He takes several nuts in his hand and then holds out both hands closed. The next in line must guess which hand contains the nuts. If he guesses correctly, he receives the nuts. If he guesses incorrectly, he has to hand over from his reserve supply the same number of nuts that It held in his hand. It then goes to the second in line, who also guesses, and so on down the line. When It reaches the foot of the line, he stays there and the next head of the line becomes It. The game proceeds until all have had a turn at being It. Then the player who has the most nuts wins the game.—*From "Children at Play in Many Lands," by Katharine Stanley Hall.*

FLOWER RELAY
(Go-oot Kyung-ju)

Out of doors   *Similar to Relay Race*
20-40 players, both boys and girls, 6-10 years

This game is suitable for play festivals, as the flower trees are decorative and lend a festive air when the relay is over.

Two trees or thick branches of trees set about ten feet apart on one side of the playing group are needed. It is best to have trees with thorns, but if these are not available, then use any tree to which flowers may be easily attached. Each player must have a good-sized real or paper flower. If the tree has no thorns, each flower must have a string or pin attached so that it may be quickly fastened to the tree.

Sides may be chosen by letting the girls and boys stand in a row and count one-two-one-two, etc., until all are numbered. The number ones form one side and the number twos the other.

The children stand one behind the other in two lines at opposite ends of the playing ground, facing the trees. Each line is just opposite the tree to which it is to attach flowers and at equal distances from it.

The leader gives a signal and the first child in each line races to his tree, attaches his flower, and takes his place near the tree but not close enough to get in the next player's way. As soon as he has taken his place after attaching his flower, the next child starts running and so on until the whole side has run.

The game is won by the side that first succeeds in attaching all its flowers to its tree so that they do not fall off.

PANGIE CHANG MAN

Indoors or out of doors   *Similar to Button, Button*
8-20 players, 8-12 years

Two teams, each with a captain, are required to play this game. These teams may be represented by lines A and B, which face each other. Halfway between the two lines is the goal. The captain of the A line hides a ring or some other small article somewhere about the person of some player in his line. Then line B tries to guess which player has the article. Three guesses are allowed. If line B succeeds in guessing correctly, it then has the ring to hide; if not, the whole line A moves forward one step and hides the ring again. Every time a line hides the ring so well that it is not found, it moves forward a step. The line that first reaches the middle line or goal wins the game.—*From "World Friends."*

BALL ROLLING
(Kong Kool-gee)

3-6 players, boys and girls, 8-12 years   *Out of doors*

The players have a small ball, such as a marble. Small holes are dug in the ground, each just large enough for the ball to drop into easily when rolled. There should be as many holes as there are players, and the holes are assigned, one to each player. Players and holes are numbered to correspond and number one starts the game. The holes should be dug in two lines, one behind the other, those in the second line being in the alternate spaces between those in the first line.

The players stand on a line from eight to ten feet from the holes and the first player rolls the ball toward the holes.

All the players watch to see into which hole the ball drops. The person into whose hole the ball goes runs and gets the ball and tries to tag one of the other players, who all run away. The person tagged rolls the ball the next time.

TOKEN GIVING
(Poong Chooge)

Indoors or out of doors   *Similar to Button, Button*
Any even number of boys or girls or both

A token, such as a stone, a coin, a ring, or a thimble is needed. Two leaders are selected and they choose sides, one by one, until all the players are taken. The two lines of players stand facing each other from three to five feet apart. The leader who had second turn in choosing sides now has first turn with the token. He goes down the line of his players, each of whom holds his hands out in front of him, ready to receive the token. The leader may give it to any one of the players on his side or he may keep it himself. The leader on the other side then tries to guess who has the token. He has three chances at guessing. If he guesses correctly, he gains the token for his side. If he fails to guess correctly in his three turns, the other side scores a point and keeps the token.

On the second trial the player next to the leader passes along his side with the token. Then the player next to the leader on the other side does the guessing. Thus each player has a turn with the token and at guessing.

The game continues as long as desired and the side having the higher score is the winner.

SEESAW

2 players   *Out of doors*

The Korean way of playing "Seesaw" may also prove of interest to boys and girls enjoying an outdoor party. A large bag is filled with sand and a broad plank is laid across this. Then two boys or two girls stand up straight, one on either end of the board. When both are ready, one jumps up; and when he comes back down on his end of the board, his partner is thrown into the air. Then the fun begins, just as in our game of "Seesaw," only in a much more exciting way!— *From "World Friends."*

Malaya

FOOTBALL
(Bola Kake)

4-6 players, boys, 12 years and up   *Out of doors*

Boys can be seen playing *"Bola Kake"* in the side streets of Singapore or even in front of the shop houses, as well as in the *kampongs* far outside any city limits on the Malay Peninsula. Malay lads use a round, light ball made of split wicker, or sometimes a shuttlecock, for this game. In this country a light rubber ball could be used.

Four or six boys, divided into equal sides, usually make up the players. The teams face each other. The ball is kicked by the bare foot across to the opposing players. The opponent is supposed to catch it on the fly with his own bare foot and then return it. Each time a player fails to catch and return the ball, a point is counted for the other side against his side. When a score that has previously been decided upon is reached, the game is over.—*Mrs. Florence Kesselring, Malay Peninsula.*

The children of Malaya use the counting out game, "Stone, Scissors, Paper," as in China. See page 40.

Syria

CHOOSING IT

When choosing a leader for tag or other games, the Syrian children form a long line, each holding the one in front of him, then all pull. The first one to break loose becomes It.—*From "Rainbow Packet" of the Presbyterian Church in the U.S.A.*

HAT TAG

Usually out of doors   *Similar to Tag*
6-20 players, boys, 8-12 years

A circle from two to three feet in diameter is drawn on the ground with a stick, or on the floor with chalk if the game is played indoors. One boy is chosen to be It and he puts his hat in the center of the circle. He stands inside the circle with one foot on the line and he may not leave the ring as long as his hat remains inside it. The others try to knock the hat out of the circle with their hands or feet. While they are doing this,

It tries to tag them. If he touches a player, that one becomes It. But if anyone succeeds in knocking the hat out of the circle without being touched, It may leave the ring and run away from the circle to tag and make It anyone whom he can catch.— *From "Rainbow Packet" of the Presbyterian Church in the U.S.A.*

BALL

Any number of players   *Usually out of doors*

In Syria each child uses his own ball for this game. There will be more fun, however, if the children play in turn and a score is kept of each player's catch.

The ball is bounced on the floor and before it is caught, the player must whirl around once. The one who can bounce the ball, whirl around, and catch it the greatest number of times without missing wins the game.—*From "Rainbow Packet" of the Presbyterian Church in the U.S.A.*

The children of Syria enjoy a game that is much like "Ear and Nose" as played in Iran. See page 57.

MARBLES

Indoors or out of doors   *Similar to Marbles*
           2 or more players, usually boys, 8-12 years

Syrian children usually use pebbles or stones for marbles in this game. Each player digs a small hole in the ground. If the game is played indoors, a small receptacle such as a tin cup or small flat tray may be used. The holes should be placed in a row very close together and the marbles are rolled into the holes. If the game is played indoors, the marbles are thrown gently into the cups. Each player has an equal number of marbles, usually three or four. He stands about eight feet away from the line of holes and tries to roll a marble into his own hole or to toss it into his own cup. He scores the number that he succeeds in getting into the cup. If he throws any marbles into another's cup, they are counted for that player. A player scores the number of marbles in his cup, whether thrown by himself or by someone else. The game may consist of one or several throws by each player; or a certain score, such as ten, may constitute a game.—*From "Rainbow Packet" of the Presbyterian Church in the U.S.A.*

Thailand

HIT THE COIN

4-20 players, 6-12 years   *Out of doors*

A long bamboo stick is driven into the ground with its top about the level of the children's eyes. A coin (say a penny) is placed on top of the stick. A child stands from eight to ten yards distant, holding his hand over one eye so he can see with only one. He walks to the stick and tries to flip off the penny with his thumb and second finger. If he hits the penny, he wins a point. If he misses, the next child has his turn. Only one turn is allowed.—*From "Rainbow Packet" of the Presbyterian Church in the U.S.A.*

TAKRAM

6-10 players, 10-14 years   *Usually out of doors*

A small, hollow reed ball is used in playing this game. A balloon or tennis ball may be substituted in this country. The players stand in a circle. One of them tosses the ball to another player, who knocks it on to another by hitting it with his head, shoulder, elbow, knee, toe, or heel. To hit the ball with a heel or head shot is regarded as a very skillful and clever play. The ball cannot be tossed with the hand except on the original play.—*From "Rainbow Packet" of the Presbyterian Church in the U.S.A.*

Turkey

PRESENTS AND PUNISHMENTS
(Hediye ve Jeza)

8-30 players, usually girls, 8-12 years   Indoors or out of doors

The player who is It kneels and puts her head into the lap of another who is seated. Thus It cannot see what is happening. The seated player makes a motion and says, "To whom will you give this?" It names someone in the room to whom she bequeaths the motion, although, of course, she has no idea what it is. For example, the seated player may make a motion of spanking and ask, "To whom will you give this?" A kiss, a frown, a kick, and any number of things can be shown by action, according to the ingenuity of the questioner. Much laughter is caused by the various "donations." When the questioner's ingenuity runs out, another takes her place.—*Miss Jessie E. Martin, Merzifon, Turkey.*

FOX AND HEN
(Tilki ve Tavuk)

Out of doors   Similar to Fox and Geese

One player is chosen to be the Fox and he selects a spot as his Den. One of the tallest players is the Hen and the other players, who are the Chickens, line up behind her, each holding onto the one in front. The Fox approaches the Hen and asks for the Chicken at the end of the line and the Hen refuses. The Hen, with her brood of Chickens following her every movement, tries to keep in front of the Fox to prevent him from getting around to the end of the line. This requires quite a lot of maneuvering and is very exciting. When the Fox succeeds in catching a Chicken, he takes him to his Den, comes back and tries for the next. Then the Hen may recover her stolen Chickens from the Den, moving over to the Den and touching them, all the while protecting those that remain. The Chicken may hold out her hand to make her recapture easier. The game goes on until the Fox has all the Chickens or until the Hen has recaptured them all.—*Miss Jessie E. Martin, Merzifon, Turkey.*

PACIFIC ISLANDS

Indonesia

A COUNTING OUT GAME
(Betten)

2 players, seeking first turns   *Indoors or out of doors*

The leaders stand facing each other, swinging their right hands behind their heads. They count together, "One, two, three, go!" On the word "go," the hands are held out in one of three signs: the thumb, the first, or the little finger may point outward. Each of these signs has a special meaning and value in the game. The thumb represents an Elephant, the first finger a Man, and the little finger an Ant. The Elephant wins over the Man because he can step on him and crush him; the Man wins over the Ant because he can so easily kill him; the Ant wins over the Elephant because he can run up his trunk and tickle him to death.

If the players happen to make the same sign, they must try again. The one who has made the winning sign has first choice.—*Miss Catherina Fruin, Holland and the United States.*

WATCHMAN
(Nachtwacht)

5-20 players, boys and girls, 6-14 years   **Indoors**

This game is played by Dutch children in Indonesia and in Holland. It must be played at night when it is dark.

One player is chosen to be It and he leaves the room. The others are given numbers from one up. They hide themselves around the room. They do not have to hide very carefully because the lights are put out. It is called back to the room, in which a gong has been placed. (A pan and spoon will do.) It strikes the gong and says, "The clock strikes one!" The child who is number one must make a noise like an animal. It must guess the name of the player making the noise. If he does not guess correctly, he must seek the player in the dark, trying to locate the spot from which the voice came. The player may not move from his place after he has made the animal noise. When the name has been guessed or the player caught, the gong is struck twice and It says, "The clock strikes two!" The child whose number is two must reply with an animal noise. So the game proceeds. The player who has not been guessed by name or caught by touching becomes It for the next game.—*Miss Catherina Fruin, Holland and the United States.*

New Guinea: Papua

STEPPING ON THE DOG
(Guan Pazek)

Boys, 9-16 years   **Out of doors**

Among the various animals and birds of the New Guinea bush, the dog is Public Enemy Number 1. When the dog accompanies his master, a Papuan hunter, on a hunting trip, he nearly always kills some wild animals or birds, or directs the attention of his master to them, so that they are killed with an arrow or spear.

The children have made up a game about the Dog and the animals and birds of the bush. It is based on the idea that the animals of the woods and two birds, the Bush Fowl and the Cassowary (nearly as large as an ostrich), get together for a bush conference and decide to meet near the village so that they can attack and perhaps kill the Dog while he is asleep.

The game is played by Papuan boys who act the roles of the different animals: Bandicoots, Field Mice, Lizards, Rabbits, etc. The three best actors, as a rule, play the roles of the Dog, the Cassowary, and the Wallaby (a small bush kangaroo).

The Dog lies asleep and the birds and animals creep close to him. Both the Cassowary and the Wallaby volunteer to kill the Dog. All the other little allies creep up from the circle around the sleeping enemy. They sing the following song repeatedly as they advance.

Bau pe wena, Kisi pe wena, Kisi Komi Komi Komi.

The two attackers advance toward the Dog, nudging each other to encourage attack. Finally the Cassowary does attack the Dog, but only awakens him. The Dog grasps and disables the Wallaby. While the tussle between the two is going on, the Cassowary is too fearful to come to his friend's aid. He runs to and fro wildly in ever widening circles in the characteristic running gait of the Cassowary, while the small animals all run for shelter in the near-by bush.

The Cassowary is really the main figure in the game. The

actor makes use of grasses and leaves to make himself look
like a Cassowary. The Wallaby and the Dog are the Cassowary's close seconds as regards acting. The little animals, too,
cause a great deal of merriment.—*E. F. Hanneman, Port
Moresby, New Guinea.*

MAILONG SERA

6-20 players, boys and girls, 8-15 years   Similar to Button, Button

The players form a ring, with one who has been chosen as
It in the center. They may stand about six to eight inches apart,
or they may be seated with their legs stretched in front of them.
They hold their arms half extended forward, palms downward.
A seashell about the size of a half dollar is passed, unseen,
from hand to hand. The players move their hands outward
and inward alternately, touching the hands of their neighbors
on either side and then bringing both of their hands together
in front of them. This movement permits the shell to be
passed surreptitiously around in the circle. It has to guess who
has the shell. If he guesses correctly, the one who had the shell
becomes It. A song, "Mailong Sera," is sung throughout the
game.—*E. F. Hanneman, Port Moresby, New Guinea.*

Mai - long se ra, mai - long se ra.
ma - la si sig - a - re, sig - ar - ig - ar - e.

Philippine Islands

CAT AND DOG
(Pusa at Aso)

10-20 players, 8-12 years   *Indoors or out of doors*

A large circle is marked on the ground or floor. At the center are placed some such articles as sticks, slippers, or wooden shoes, representing bones. One player is chosen as Dog and stays inside the circle guarding the bones. The other players, who are Cats, stay outside the circle. It is the object of the Cats to take the bones from the Dog without being tagged or touched by him. The Dog may tag the Cats with his feet or his hands, but he must remain seated by the bones.

The Cats may tease him by stepping in and out of the circle. While he is busy trying to tag some of the Cats, others attempt to steal the bones. If the Cats succeed in taking all the bones from the Dog without being tagged, the same player remains as Dog for the next game. If he succeeds in tagging any one of the Cats, the one tagged becomes the Dog of the next game.
—From "Filipino Playmates," by Jean Moore Cavell.

DAY AND NIGHT

Indoors or out of doors   *Similar to Tag*
10-40 players, 8-12 years

A soft, flat slipper is needed for this game. The children are divided into two teams, with a captain for each. One team is called Day and the other Night. Two parallel lines are drawn some twenty feet apart. The members of the Day team stand along one line and those of the Night team along the other. One of the captains takes the soft slipper and, standing between the two teams, tosses it into the air. As soon as the slipper lands, both teams must run from their line to the opposite line. If it lands open side up, the Days try to catch the Nights; if sole side up, the Nights try to catch the Days. If a player gets safely to the opposite side, he remains with his team; but if caught, he must go over to the opposing team. The game continues until all the players are on one side or the other. The captains take turns in tossing the shoe and do not participate in the catch.—*From "Jewels the Giant Dropped," by Edith Eberle and Grace W. McGavran.*

TAG
(Dakpanay)

Indoors or out of doors   *Similar to Tag*
3-20 players, boys and girls

The ground or floor is marked off with from three to five circles. The size of the circles varies according to the number of players. Usually one large circle is drawn as a resting place for the circle players. The circles may be drawn close to each other or they may be far apart.

One player is chosen to be the Chaser. The rest are circle players. The Chaser stays outside the circles and the others stay inside. The object is for the Chaser to tag any of the circle players. The circle players can transfer from one circle to another, but the Chaser is not allowed to step inside or to run across any circle.

In order to confuse the Chaser, the circle players scatter and occupy all the circles and stay near the circumference of the circle. As soon as the Chaser comes near, they run to another circle or to the big circle. In this case the Chaser has a hard time to tag them. A player tagged by the Chaser exchanges places with him, becoming the new Chaser.—*From "Filipino Playmates," by Jean Moore Cavell.*

STICKS

6-20 players, 8-10 years   *Indoors or out of doors*

With a piece of chalk, mark a ring on the floor about eighteen inches or two feet in diameter. Place about six sticks within the circle, and give each player two stones. The players in turn attempt to knock the sticks out of the circle by hitting them with the stones. The players can be lined up into two or more teams. Each team then plays in turn, player for player. A player scores five for each stick he knocks out of the circle. The players, in throwing, stand about ten feet away from the circle.— *From "Jewels the Giant Dropped," by Edith Eberle and Grace W. McGavran.*

ILOCANO BALL

Boys and men   *Out of doors*

This is an old game of the Filipino people and is played by boys and men. They are accustomed to collect on street corners or in vacant lots where there is plenty of space. The cool of the evening is the favorite time for the game.

The ball is made of rattan, hollow, with open spaces between the weaving, so that it is very light. It is tossed into the air and the fun has begun. In this country a lightweight rubber ball may be used. The players keep the ball in motion by kicking it with the sole of the foot. It must never be touched by another part of the body. Considerable skill is required to twist the foot into the correct position to toss the ball with the sole. It is difficult, too, to keep balanced in the rapid movement and intricate twisting that is required. The point is to keep the ball in motion as long as possible. When it touches the ground, it is tossed into the air again, and the game begins once more. Points are scored every time the ball is successfully kicked.

There are variations of the game in which the elbow or the heel is used for tossing the ball.—*From "Jewels the Giant Dropped," by Edith Eberle and Grace W. McGavran.*

HIDE AND SEEK
(Taguan)

2-20 players, 6-10 years   *Indoors or out of doors*

One player is chosen to be It. He remains at a base determined by all the players. His eyes are closed or his face covered. The other players then hide. When securely hidden, they call out, *"Pakit"* (You're It!). It then goes in search of them. Those who are hiding may repeat the call at their discretion.

The game ends when all the players are found. The player who is first found will be It in the next game.—*From "Filipino Playmates," by Jean Moore Cavell.*

GRAB THE HUSK
(Sambunot)

10-30 players, 10-14 years   *Indoors or out of doors*

The ground or the floor of the gymnasium is divided into two equal parts with a small hole dug or a circle drawn at the center of a neutral line. A coconut husk is placed in the hole. In this country a corn husk or a piece of cloth might be used.

Two goal lines are drawn, parallel to the central line and at an equal distance from it, say thirty feet. The players are divided into two teams of equal numbers. Each team lines up along one of the goal lines. At the signal "Go!" the players of both teams rush to the neutral line to grab the husk. The player who succeeds turns and tries to take the husk back to his own goal line. The players of the other team try their best to catch him and take the husk away from him. The players of his own side try to protect him. The one who holds the husk may not pass it to anyone else, though it may be taken from him. The team whose player succeeds in reaching the home goal line with the husk is the winner.—*From "Filipino Playmates," by Jean Moore Cavell.*

PANTALUNTUN

10-30 players, boys and girls, 10-14 years   Indoors or out of doors

Two captains are chosen, and they in turn choose sides. In the Philippine Islands, the children play in the dusty streets, first sprinkling water on the dust so that they can mark lines in it. In this country lines may be made on the floor or ground.

A long main line is drawn and a number of cross lines, ten to fifteen feet long, are marked along it, at right angles to it and about five feet apart. There should be as many cross lines as there are players. The captain moves along the main line.

Each player takes his place on some cross line and he may move anywhere along that line. No player may step off his particular line. Team A arranges its men along the lines. At a given signal, Team B attempts to go from one end of the field to the other and then back again, running around one end of one cross line and the other end of the next. They may cross the main line but not those at right angles to it. The players along the lines try to touch them as they run. As soon as one player is touched by a player on the lines, a point is scored for Team A and the teams change positions, Team B taking its place on the lines. If, on the other hand, all the players of Team B get through untouched, a point is scored by that side, and a second attempt is made by them.—*From "Jewels the Giant Dropped," by Edith Eberle and Grace W. McGavran.*

Games from Latin America

THE children of Latin America love to sing as they play their games. So you will find a number of songs included in the games from Latin America. The music is given for some of the songs; but it has not been possible to include music for all. In games where the music is not given, the children may repeat together the words of the song, or set it to music with which they are familiar.

Though the games are located in the various countries of Latin America, many of them are played in *all* the countries. For instance, the game "A Piñata," which appears under the heading of Nicaragua, is very popular in Mexico, and is played in other countries as well. Sometimes the games vary slightly from country to country. A few of these variations are given.

In playing the games with the children, it would be well to note the similarities to games of their own and thus to emphasize the likenesses among boys and girls in all countries. It would be interesting to discuss how the character and customs of a country are apparent in the games that are played in it. For instance, the names of the common animals and flowers often appear in many of the games. The children may enjoy hearing the native title of the game and working out the meaning of the different words. In some of the games in this section, the Spanish words of the game are given. Sometimes the children may play the game in Spanish.

The playing of these games from other countries should give the children a feeling of fellowship with the boys and girls of Latin America.

THE CARIBBEAN ISLANDS

Cuba

THE SHEPHERDESS AND THE CAT

8-20 players, usually girls, 6-10 years   *Indoors or out of doors*

Two children are chosen to take the parts of the Shepherdess and the Cat. The others move in a ring around them, holding hands as they circle and sing. The Shepherdess carries out the action suggested in the song and the Cat watches her and follows her. During the last verse, the Cat scratches at the Shepherdess, who pretends to cut off its tail.

> There was a little shepherdess,
> Laran, laran, larock;
> There was a little shepherdess,
> A-watching of her flock.
>
> With goats' milk, with goats' milk,
> Laran, laran, lareeze;
> With goats' milk, with goats' milk,
> She made a little cheese.
>
> The little cat was watching her,
> Laran, laran, larize;
> The little cat was watching her,
> With hungry, longing eyes.
>
> If you show me a claw,
> Laran, laran, larail;
> With your hungry maw, if you show me a claw,
> I'll cut off your wriggling tail.
>
> She showed me her claw,
> Laran, laran, larail;
> She showed me her claw, with her hungry maw,
> And I cut off her wriggling tail.
>
> —*W. W. Steel.*

THE FOUNTAIN
(La Fuente)

Indoors or out of doors   *Similar to London Bridge*
8-20 players, usually girls, 6-10 years

Two little girls are chosen to form an arch, and they each
secretly take the name of a flower; for example, rose and
jasmine. They hold up their joined hands to make an arch.
The other children pass under the arch in a long line, each
girl holding the skirt of the one in front. They sing as they
march:

> Skip lively now, skip lively now,
> The fountain has been broken.

Then the two girls who are making the arch sing the next
two lines:

> Skip lively now, skip lively now,
> We'll have to have it mended.

The ones who are marching sing:

> Skip lively now, skip lively now,
> What shall we use for money?

The arch-makers sing:

> Skip lively now, skip lively now,
> We'll have to use an eggshell.

Then everybody sings the last four lines of the song together:

> Oh me, oh me, oh my,
> The queen will come today.
> The ones in front may all pass by
> But the last one has to stay.

Everybody passes under the arch except the last one in the line, who is caught. She is asked to choose which flower she will have. After her choice, she goes to stand behind the girl whose flower she has selected, watching the game and taking part in the singing.

Over and over the children sing and each time the last in line chooses her side. When all have made choice, each girl puts her arms around the waist of the one in front. Then the two sides pull hard to see which is stronger, just as in "London Bridge."—*From "Carmita of Cuba," by Marjorie Jacob Caudill.*

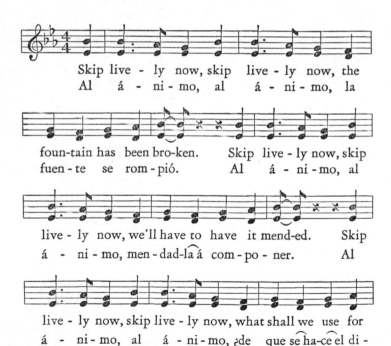

Skip live - ly now, skip   live - ly now, the
Al   á - ni - mo,   al   á - ni - mo,   la

foun-tain has been bro-ken.   Skip live - ly now, skip
fuen - te   se rom - pió.   Al   á - ni - mo, al

live - ly now, we'll have to have it mend-ed.   Skip
á - ni - mo, men - dad-lá á com - po - ner.   Al

live - ly now, skip live - ly now, what shall we use for
á - ni - mo, al á - ni - mo, ¿de que se ha-ce el di -

mon-ey? Skip live - ly now, skip live - ly now, we'll
ne - ro? Al á - ni - mo, al á - ni - mo, de

have to use an egg-shell. Oh me, oh me, oh my, the
cas - ca - ra de hue-vo. U - ri, u - ri, u - rai, la

queen will come to - day. The ones in front may
rei - na va á pa - sar. Los del an - te cor - ren

all pass by but the last one has to stay.
mu - cho y el de a - tras se que - da - rá.

THE HAWK
(El Gavilán)

Indoors or out of doors   *Similar to Fox and Geese*
5-20 players, usually girls, 8-12 years

One player takes the part of the Hawk and stands with arms outstretched. Another player is the Mother and the rest are Chickens. The Mother walks up and down in front of the Hawk with her flock of Chickens behind her, each holding on to the skirt of the one in front. All the Chickens sing,

To the fierce hawk what will they give?
Just quail and bread as sure as I live.
Not another thing upon my life
Unless it be a handsome wife.

Then the Mother calls to the Chicken at the end of the line, "Ladybug, Ladybug, there behind," to which the last Chicken replies, "What does my mother wish?" The Mother asks, "Is the Hawk dead or alive?" The last Chicken approaches the Hawk, which remains very still. "Dead," calls the last Chicken and returns to the line.

The Chickens all sing their verse over again and the dialogue between Mother and last Chicken begins over again. This time the Hawk acts out the sharpening of a knife and this the last Chicken reports to the Mother. The singing of the refrain and repeating of the dialogue goes on through the stages of shutting the door, coming down the stairs, and so on, until the Mother asks the Hawk, "What do you want?" The Hawk replies, "To eat a little Chicken." The Mother says, "Catch her if you can." An exciting chase after the last Chicken in the line begins with the Mother protecting her children by outspread arms. If the Hawk succeeds in catching the last Chicken, the one caught must take the Hawk's place and the game begins again.—*W. W. Steel*.

"The Spotted Bird" (see page 103) is also played in Cuba.

COUNTING OUT RHYMES

These are three rhymes used in counting out by the children of Cuba.

Little white dove,
Tell me the truth,
Is it this, or this,
Or *this,* forsooth?

Guinda, cherries,
Strawberry vines and berries,
Let me open . . . this.

Tita, tita, tariton,
Three hens and one capon;
The capon is dead;
The hens in the garden bed,
Ras riis, it must be . . . *this*.
　　　　　　　　　—W. W. Steel.

Puerto Rico

ONIONS FOR MOTHER
(Cebollas para Mamá)

5-20 players, 8-12 years　　　　　　　　　　　*Out of doors*

One player is chosen to be It, another to be the Trunk. All the others are Onions. The Trunk puts his hands around a tree or a post or something that is strong, which thus becomes his Home. The other players stand in a line behind him, each one with his arms around the waist of the one in front. The Trunk is supposed to be owner of the Onions, which are considered to be good for soup.

It now comes to the Trunk and says, "May I have an onion for Mother's soup?"

Trunk says, "What became of the one I sent yesterday?"

It answers, "The rats ate it all."

Then the Trunk says, "Take the one you prefer."

It goes down the line of players, touching each one on the head in turn and saying about each, "This one is no good," until he reaches the last player in the line. "This is the best onion for soup," he says. He takes hold of the last player and pulls and tugs until he gets him away from the line.

The players hold on to each other as tightly as they can.

When It gets the last player in the line, he takes him to his side. Then he goes to the Trunk and begins asking all over again. He continues until all the Onions have been taken over to his side. Now it happens that the Onions are changed into Dogs.

It goes to the Trunk saying, "Mother wants you to have soup with her."

The Trunk says, "No, I hear you have many dogs at home."

"Come, I'll remove their teeth," says It. He goes to his side and claps his hands in front of each Dog. Then he comes back to the Trunk and repeats the invitation. This time the Trunk accepts. As he nears It's side, all the Dogs start barking. The Trunk starts to run and all the dogs go after him. If he is caught before reaching his Home, he stays as the Trunk for the next game. If he escapes, someone else is chosen to be the Trunk.—*Señorita Ruth Maldonado, Puerto Rico.*

THE CAT AND THE MOUSE
(El Gato y el Ratón)

Indoors or out of doors   *Similar to Cat and Rat*
10-30 players, 5-8 years

The children name two players to be the Cat and the Mouse. The Mouse stands inside the circle. The Cat runs around outside the circle and tries to break through the clasped hands of the players to catch the Mouse. If he should get in, then the children decide whether they will allow the Mouse to escape by raising their arms to let him get out of the circle away from the Cat. When the Mouse is caught, two other children are named as Cat and Mouse and the game begins again.—*Señora Inés Quiles, Puerto Rico.*

THE STICK
(El Palo)

Out of doors   *Similar to Hide and Seek*
5-20 players, 8-12 years

A medium-sized stick is needed. One of the players is chosen to be It. He throws the stick as far as he can. He goes after the stick, picks it up and carries it to a goal that has been decided upon by all the players. While he does so, the players hide. It stands at goal, holding his stick and trying to see the hidden players. If he sees one, he calls, "I see (name of child) and hold my stick." The child who is named comes out and waits for the others to be called. If everyone is seen and called, the first to be mentioned becomes the next It.

If It cannot see the players, he must leave the stick at goal and go in search of them. If one of the hidden players gets to the stick without being seen by It, he holds the stick and shouts, "Freed!" This shout saves all the players who have already been caught. If all the players are freed, the same child must be It for a second turn.

If It sees a player running to goal, he must try to reach the stick at goal before the player, and thus count him caught.
—*Señorita Ruth Maldonado, Puerto Rico.*

GIVE ME A LIGHT
(Por Aquí Hay Candela)

Indoors or out of doors   *Similar to Pussy Wants a Corner*
10-30 players, 6-9 years

The children form a circle or a square, with four or five feet between each player. The child who has been chosen It stands in the center. It goes up to a child in the circle and says, "Give me a light from your fire." The child questioned replies, "The fire is burning over there," pointing to another child in the circle. It goes to the child pointed out and repeats the question, receiving the same reply. In the meantime, the children in the circle are changing places with each other. If It can find a vacant place, he stands there and the extra child becomes It. Or, if he catches a child running, the one caught becomes It.—*Señorita María Escobar, Puerto Rico.*

THE COLORED RIBBONS
(Las Cintas en Colores)

10-30 players, 8-12 years   *Indoors or out of doors*

Two players are needed to act out the parts of the Angel and the Bad Man, and one to name the Ribbons. The players form a circle. The child selected to name the Ribbons whispers to each player in turn the color of ribbon which he is to represent. The colors must be kept a secret. The Angel comes into the circle and the children all cry, "Angel, what do you wish?" The Angel replies, "I wish many colored ribbons." The one who named the Ribbons then asks the question, "What color ribbon do you need?" The Angel then goes up to a child and names a color. If the guess is correct, the child leaves the circle and stands behind the Angel. The Angel then goes to another child and guesses the name of his color. The same procedure is repeated until the Angel misses a guess, after which he and his colors must leave the circle. Then the Bad Man comes running and shouting and the children act as if they are afraid and cross their fingers as they ask the question, "What do you wish?" The Bad Man replies, "I wish many colored ribbons." He then guesses the colors in the same way as the Angel. When he misses, he leaves the circle with his colors, and the Angel returns. The game continues until all the children have been called. Then the Bad Man tries to catch the children who are behind the Angel and they endeavor not to be caught. The Angel tries to get the children behind the Bad Man. The game is to see which side can get the most Ribbons.—*Señorita Petronila Nieves and Señora Inés Quiles, Puerto Rico.*

THE STONES
(Las Piedras)

10-20 players, 8-12 years   *Out of doors*

The children are divided into two teams of equal size, and each team selects a captain. The two teams then line up facing each other, three to six feet apart. Each team has a large stone and a small stone. The two large stones are placed side by side, along a starting line drawn an equal distance from the opposing sides and at right angles to them. Each captain holds one of the small stones. The players hold their hands behind their backs. The captain of Team One moves along behind his line of players and hides the small stone in the hand of one member of his team, being careful not to disclose by his action to whom he has given it. He then gives the command, "Hands in front." All the players hold their closed hands out in front of them. The captain of Team Two tries to guess which player holds the small stone. If he guesses correctly, the child holding the stone hops to the large stone of the opposing team and moves it with his hand a foot away from its starting line, and then hops back to his place in the line after giving the small stone to his captain. The play procceds as before, the captain of Team Two continuing his guessing until he misses. At each correct guess, a child hops to the stone and moves it a foot farther along in a line parallel to the children. When the captain misses a guess, then the other team plays. The game is to see which team can move the large stone the farthest through the correct guessing of its captain.—*Señorita Petronila Nieves and Señora Inés Quiles, Puerto Rico.*

Trinidad

Though Trinidad does not belong to the Latin American groups, it lies in the Caribbean area and so is included here.

A COUNTING OUT GAME

One player stands with a hand held out, palm down, breast high. The other players hold their pointer fingers under the palm, touching it. The player who is holding out his hand repeats this rhyme,

> Ziggeddy, ziggeddy,
> Marble stone,
> Pointer, pointer, bouff!
> Kisskillindy, kisskillindy,
> Pa . . . Pa . . . poriff!

At the last word the reciter grabs at the touching fingers, which are hastily pulled away. The player whose finger is caught becomes It.—*From "A Highway of Friendship," by Isabel G. Uren.*

TREE-YEAR
(Trier)

Indoors or out of doors   *Similar to Jackstones*
2-10 players, 8-12 years

Part I decides the order in which the players shall take part in the game. Part II is the game itself.

PART I. The game is played with five small stones of uneven surface. The first player holds them in her palm, throws her stones up and catches as many of them as she can on the back of her hand. She throws up the remaining ones from the back of her hand and catches them in her palm. If she drops any in this back-of-hand-to-palm throw, she is "out." If not, she counts the number of stones she now holds as her score for the first toss. She makes the tosses a second and a third time in the same way, adding her points together at the end of each toss. But if at any time she drops a stone, in tossing from the back of the hand to the palm, she is "out," and her score is nothing.

All the players in turn have their chance at three tosses of the stones. At the conclusion of the tosses, the scores are compared. The one with the highest score takes the first turn in Part II and the others follow according to their scores.

PART II. The first player takes the five stones in her palm as before, tosses and catches as many as possible on the back of her hand. She tosses again and must catch all in her palm. If she misses any, she is "out," and her score is nothing. If she does not miss, she puts down all the stones but one. She tosses the one, picks up one of the stones on the ground and catches the one she tossed. She tosses again and picks up another and so on, until all are gathered up. If two stones are lying close together on the ground, she must pick up both at one toss, one after the other. That is, she must not touch one while picking up another, or she is "out." If she misses catching the toss while picking up one, she is "out."

If she picks up all the stones correctly, she counts one point. She repeats the process over and over up to twelve times. If she has been successful, she counts twelve and passes the stones to the player who has second turn. The process of throwing is repeated. When all have played, the one with the lowest score puts her hand on the ground. The two who did best pinch the back of her hand lightly.—*From "A Highway of Friendship," by Isabel G. Uren.*

MIDDLE AMERICA

Mexico

THE THREE GENTLE RAPS
(Los Tres Toquecitos)

Indoors or out of doors   *Similar to Hide and Seek*
5-20 players, 8-12 years

The player who is It becomes the Porter and he stands beside the goal, which is called the Door. He shuts his eyes and counts slowly from one to twenty, while the other players go and hide. When he has finished counting, the Porter goes in search of the others, always trying to keep close to his Door. The hidden players try to sneak closer and closer to the Door without being seen. When one of them gets close enough, he runs to the Door and raps three times, saying, "One, two, three for me." This being done, he is safe, but now he becomes the Porter's helper and must aid him at his job. If he or the Porter sees another child, the one who sees him first runs to the Door and raps three times, counting, "One, two, three for (Joe or Mary or whoever it is)." If the player can run fast enough to get to the goal first and rap on it three times, he is safe. As soon as one player is caught, he becomes the next Porter. The others are called for a new game.—*Señorita Rosa Ruíz de la Peña, Mexico City*.

THE RIBBONS
(Los Listones)

10-20 players, 8-12 years   *Indoors or out of doors*

One of the players is chosen to be the Buyer, another the Seller, and the others become Ribbons. The Buyer goes a short distance away from the group so that he cannot overhear what is said. The Seller tells every one of the Ribbons what his color is, trying to select colors that will be hard to guess. This being done, the players sit down and the Seller stands beside them. At a call from the Seller, the Buyer comes back, hopping on one foot. He stops in front of the Seller and makes believe that he is rapping at a door. Then the following dialogue takes place:

BUYER: Rap, rap.   SELLER: Who is it?
BUYER: Old Agnes.   SELLER: What does she want?
BUYER: To buy a ribbon.   SELLER: What color?

Here the Buyer mentions a color. If he guesses correctly the color of any player in the group, that player must go with him. If he guesses wrong, he makes another try. He has as many tries as there are players. When all the colors or most of them have been guessed, two others become Buyer and Seller.—*Señorita Rosa Ruíz de la Peña, Mexico City.*

THE LITTLE PARROT
(El Periquito)

8-30 players, 6-10 years   *Indoors or out of doors*

All the players are seated in a ring. One of them is chosen to start the game. He holds in his hand something small such as a little stone or a match. He turns to the player on the right and says very seriously, "Won't you buy this little parrot?" The other asks, "Does it bite?" The first answers, "No, it does not bite." Then he gives the small stone or other object to the player on his right. The new owner turns to the one on his right and asks the same questions of the third player; but when he is asked if the parrot bites, he must not answer. He must then turn to the first player and ask, "Does it bite?" When he receives the answer, "No, it does not bite," he repeats this to the third player and gives the stone to him. The game goes on in this way, with the question, "Does it bite?" always being referred back from child to child, around the circle, to the first player for the answer. The answer is likewise passed from player to player back to the one who then holds the small stone or object. The one who forgets to pass along the dialogue or who laughs must pay a forfeit.—*Señorita Rosa Ruíz de la Peña, Mexico City.*

THE STREET OF THE TOMPEATE
(La Calle del Tompeate)

Indoors or out of doors   *Similar to Fox and Geese*
8-20 players, 8-12 years

Two players are selected to be the Hen and the Coyote. The other players are the Chicks. The Chicks form a line, one behind the other, each putting his hands on either side of the waist of the player in front. The Hen is at the head of the line. The Coyote goes to the Hen and says, "Where is the street of the Tompeate?" (*A tompeate* is a kind of basket without a handle.) The Hen points to the right and says, "Right here." The Coyote says, "No, they told me that it is right here." He tries to go to the left in order to catch one of the Chicks. The Hen turns to the left with all the Chicks, protecting them. The Coyote then runs to the right, trying always to catch the last Chick in the line.

The Hen and the Chicks twist and turn in the line, trying to avoid the Coyote. If the Coyote succeeds in catching the last Chick, he places him in back of him and the dialogue and play are repeated. If the line breaks, all the players below the break go with the Coyote. The game ends when all the Chicks have been caught, including the Hen.—*Señorita Rosa Ruíz de la Peña, Mexico City.*

BREAD AND CHEESE
(Pan y Queso)

Indoors or out of doors   *Similar to Pussy Wants a Corner*
8-20 players, 8-12 years

One player is chosen to be the Buyer. The others form themselves into a ring, or better, a square, standing about twelve feet apart from each other, the Buyer being in the center. The Buyer goes to one of the children and asks, "Where do they sell bread and cheese?" The other answers, pointing to one of the most distant players, "There, and it is very hard." The Buyer goes to the player who has been pointed out, in order to ask the same question. Meanwhile the one who was questioned changes places with the one directly opposite him in the circle or the square. If the Buyer moves rapidly and gets in one of the empty spaces before either of the two who are changing places, he remains there. The one who is left without a place becomes the Buyer.— *Señorita Rosa Ruíz de la Peña, Mexico City.*

THE SPOTTED BIRD
(La Pájara Pinta)

7-20 players, 6-12 years   *Indoors or out of doors*

One child is chosen to be the Spotted Bird. He stands in the center of a circle formed by the others, who move around him holding hands and singing the first verse of the song.

At the end of the verse, the child in the center kneels at the feet of his "love," one of the children in the circle. Standing still, the children sing the second verse of the song.

The child chosen by the Spotted Bird now stands in the center of the circle and the child who chose him returns to the circle. The singing is repeated until each child in the circle has had a turn at being the Spotted Bird.

A gay lit - tle spot - ted bird sat High
I kneel at the feet of my dear love And

up - on a green le - mon tree. Be -
of - fer my true loy - al - ty. With my

neath one small wing he'd a let - ter; In his
right hand, my left hand I pledge love to the

beak was a flow - er for thee.
bird in the green le - mon tree.

Oh, tell me, when will I see my love?

This game is also played in Cuba with slight variations in the words.—*From "Rafael and Consuelo," by Florence Crannell Means and Harriet L. Fullen.*

The game "A Piñata" (see page 109) is widely used in Mexico.

DOÑA BLANCA
(Lady Blanche)

6-20 players, usually girls, 8-12 years   *Indoors or out of doors*

One of the players, a girl, is Doña Blanca, another Jicotillo (he-ko-tee′yo), which means hornet. The rest, joining hands, form a ring and Doña Blanca stands in the center. Jicotillo stays at a short distance from the ring. The players begin to move to their right, singing the first verse of the song. The group stops moving and Doña Blanca sings the first two lines of the second verse. And then Jicotillo answers by singing the last two lines of the second verse.

Do - ña Blan - ca is al - ways guard - ed
Who is the smart brave Ji - co - til - lo

By great gold and sil - ver pil - lars.
That is af - ter Do - ña Blan - ca?

Let us break one of these pil - lars, then we'll
I'm the smart brave Ji - co - til - lo that is

look at Doñ - a Blan - ca.
af - ter Doñ - a Blan - ca.

After singing, Jicotillo goes to the ring and begins to ask, "Of what is this pillar made?" trying to separate the hands of the players. If they answer, "Of gold" (or of brass, or of any other strong material), Jicotillo goes to another "pillar," and then to another until someone answers, "It is made of paper" (or of flowers or of any other weak material). Then he breaks the "pillar" and goes into the ring trying to catch Doña Blanca. She runs out with Jicotillo after her. If he catches Doña Blanca, two other players become Doña Blanca and Jicotillo. If he fails, another girl takes the place of Doña Blanca, but Jicotillo has to have another turn.—*Señorita Rosa Ruiz de la Peña, Mexico City.*

GODFATHERS
(Compradritos)

10-30 boys and girls, 10-12 years   *Indoors or out of doors*

The girls form a line on one side of the room, and the boys on the other side. One of the girls is chosen to be It. She whispers secretly to each girl the name of one of the boys opposite. The first boy in the line approaches one of the girls, hand extended, and greets her. "How do you do, Godmother?" If he has chosen the girl who has been given his name, she will take his hand and shake it, answering, "How do you do, Godfather?" Then she will exchange places with him in the line. If, however, she has not been given his name, she will refuse his hand and answer, "I do not know you," and he will return to his place. The next boy in the line takes his turn. The play continues until all the girls have taken places in the boys' line. Then the girls will approach the boys, trying to find their "Godfathers" until all places have again been exchanged.—*Mrs. John R. Kempers, Tuxtla Gutierrez, Chiapas, Mexico.*

Nicaragua

SR. CARACOL
(Mr. Snail)

5-15 players, 6-8 years   *Indoors or out of doors*

There are an uneven number of players; an even number in a circle clasping hands and the odd one standing in the center being Sr. Caracol. As the children in the circle sing, they march or skip around Sr. Caracol.

Little Caracol is dancing—Sr. Caracol, Sr. Caracol.
Let us give him what is due him—Sr. Caracol, Sr. Caracol.
  (All bow to center.)
Let us turn our backs upon him, Sr. Caracol, Sr. Caracol.
  (All turn from center.)
Let us face again our hero, Sr. Caracol, Sr. Caracol.
  (All face center again.)
Let us hunt our wedding partner, Sr. Caracol, Sr. Caracol.

Each player claps both hands or embraces another player. Sr. Caracol finds a partner among those in the circle. As there are an even number of players in the circle when Sr. Caracol chooses his partner, one player is left without a partner. That player takes his place in the center and becomes Sr. Caracol.—*Miss Mary Butler, Managua, Nicaragua.*

Lit - tle   Ca - ra - col   is   danc - ing

Se - ñor Ca - ra - col,   Se - ñor   Ca - ra - col.

MARTINILLO

8-20 players, 9-12 years   *Indoors or out of doors*

After singing games, the next favorites with Latin American children are dialogue games. The game "Martinillo" (mar-tee-nee'yo) is an example. The players form a circle. One player is chosen to be It and another to be Martinillo. It has a stick or strap, and he takes his place outside the circle. Martinillo runs around the outside of the circle and the child with the stick chases him, trying to hit him. The following conversation takes place between the two as they run:

IT: "Martinillo."

MARTINILLO: "Yes, Sir."

IT: "Where is the little mule?"

MARTINILLO: "I sold it."

IT: "Where is the money?"

MARTINILLO: "I gambled it away."

IT: "Where are the dice?"

MARTINILLO: "I burned them."

IT: "Where are the ashes?"

MARTINILLO: "On your shirt."

IT: "Where is the salt?"

MARTINILLO: "In its proper place."

At this, Martinillo and It both try to get to the place formerly occupied by Martinillo. All the time It is trying to hit Martinillo with the stick. If Martinillo gets to his place first, another player is chosen to run. If It gets there first, Martinillo takes the stick and assumes the role of It, another player being chosen to take Martinillo's place.

The conversation has a rhythm in Spanish, which is, of course, lost in the translation into English.—*Miss Mary Butler, Managua, Nicaragua.*

A PIÑATA

5-30 players   *Children's party*

Invited to a *piñata* party! Sure of a good time!

The *piñata* (peen-yah'tah) is made of a clay jar covered with crepe paper to represent an animal, bird, or flower, or anything attractive. It is suspended from the ceiling by a pulley cord and is lowered to the child's reach. The child is blindfolded but stays near so he knows exactly where to strike. Armed with a stick, he attempts to break the *piñata;* but just as he strikes, the *piñata* is pulled out of his reach. Then it is lowered again, ready for the next strike. Each child has a trial or two and then another is given a chance. The person managing the rope must be careful to keep the *piñata* out of reach until many have had a chance; yet for the sake of interest of the others watching, he tries to keep as near the stick as is safe. This game may continue for a half or three-quarters of an hour. Finally the *piñata* is left near enough to be struck. The first strike may break it, but it will probably take several hard strokes. When it breaks, out come confetti, popcorn, candies, and sometimes pennies or half pennies. Everyone scrambles to get all he can. Such excitement as each child fills his little fists with sweets and money!
—*Miss Mary Butler, Managua, Nicaragua.*

SOUTH AMERICA

Argentina

THE MAN, THE TIGER, AND THE GUN
(El Hombre, el Tigre, y el Fusil)

6-30 players, 10-16 years   *Out of doors*

This game was introduced into Argentina by a Peruvian student.

The players are divided into two equal groups, which stand facing each other. It is well to have a referee to give signals and keep score.

The following combinations must be understood:

The tiger kills the man, therefore the tiger wins.

The gun shoots the tiger, therefore the gun wins.

The man operates the gun, therefore the man wins.

The two groups of players go into huddles and secretly decide what they are going to represent, Tiger, Gun, or Man. Then they turn facing each other, and at a signal from the referee, each represents what has been agreed upon. If the A's represent Man and the B's represent Tiger, the B's win a point. If the A's represent Gun, and the B's represent Man, the B's win again. If the A's represent Gun and B's represent Tiger, the B's lose. If both should choose to represent Tiger, for example, the outcome is a tie and no one scores.

All this must go very snappily until one group has gained ten points, or the score that has been decided upon.

But a most important consideration is the pantomime. The players one and all must pantomime whatever they choose to represent. Man crosses his arms over his chest in a haughty attitude. Tiger raises his hands shoulder high and shows his claws and his teeth also. The Gun is usually represented by holding one arm out like a barrel of a gun, the right forefinger on the trigger in the attitude of sighting.—*Mrs. Vera L. Stockwell, Buenos Aires, Argentina.*

A FINE DAY TO YOU, YOUR LORDSHIP
(Muy Buen Día, Su Señoría)

8-20 players, usually girls, 8-12 years   *Indoors or out of doors*
Similar to Here Comes a Knight a-Riding

This game is a dialogue ritual which has perhaps come down from feudal times. It may be sung to the same tune as "Here Comes a Knight a-Riding," since the music used in Argentina is not available.

The children form in two lines, facing each other, about eight steps apart. One line represents His Lordship's side and the other the side of the Mother, whose daughter is being sought. First one side advances and retreats, then the other, marching forward as they sing a line of the song and retreating on the refrain. The refrain, "Man tan tiru liru la!" (maan-taan-tee-roo-lee-roo-lah) is sung after each line of the song.

A fine day to you, your Lordship.
Man tan tiru liru la!
What were you wanting, Lordship? *(Refrain)*
I was wanting one of your daughters. *(Refrain)*
Which one was your Lordship wanting? *(Refrain)*
I was wanting the one named ———. *(Refrain)*
What trade shall we now give her? *(Refain)*
We shall give her that of servant (or teacher, pianist, barber, etc.).
    (Refrain)
But she says she does not like that. *(Refrain)*
We shall give her that of ———. *(Refrain)*
She says that she likes that trade. *(Refrain)*

Before naming the occupation of the Daughter, whose services are requested, His Lordship's side consults together. The Mother's side also consults the child chosen, as to whether the occupation is agreeable or not. At the end of the song, His Lordship's group become the Mother's and vice versa, and the game is played over again.—*Miss Muriel David, Buenos Aires, Argentina.*

MISTER NOAH HAD AN ARK
(En el Arca de Noe)

6-20 players, 6-10 years   *Indoors or out of doors*

The children form a circle, holding hands. One child or the leader is in the center of the circle. During the singing of the first verse, the children march or skip around the circle, coming to a stop at the end of the last line. During the second verse the sounds of animal calls are imitated, the one in the center directing the rest in the mimicry. At the end of the last line of the second verse, the children all clap their hands and pirouette one complete turn.

> Mister Noah had an ark
> Big enough for everybody;
> Mister Noah had an ark,
> Big enough for you and me.
>
> The rooster he crowed this way (all crow),
> And then he crowed this way (all crow).
> Mister Noah had an ark,
> Big enough for you and me.

Other verses may be added to include chickens cackling, ducks and drakes quacking, spotted cows mooing, collie dog barking, etc. Since the music used in Argentina is not available, it is suggested that the words be sung to the familiar tune, "On the Bridge of Avignon."—*Miss Muriel David, Buenos Aires, Argentina.*

RING AROUND A ROSY
(A la Rueda Rueda)

6-15 players, 6-8 years   *Indoors or out of doors*

The children form a circle, holding hands and moving around as they sing. At the word "whack," they stop circling with a jump. On the words "girl" and "maripe," they jump again. On the word "pat," they all squat on their heels. The verse is sung or chanted over and over and its almost literal translation is as follows:

> Circle, circle, circle,
> Of bread and cinnamon;
> Along came the teacher,
> Gave me a *whack*.
> What a smart little *girl!*
> *Maripe* (mah-ree′pay), *maripe*
> I sat down *pat!*
> —*Miss Muriel David, Buenos Aires, Argentina.*

RICE PUDDING
(Arroz con Leche)

6-20 players, 6-10 years   *Indoors or out of doors*

The players join hands, forming a circle, and skip toward the left as they sing. The song is the important thing. A child who is It stands in the center and on the last line of the song chooses a Señorita to marry. As the song ends, the child who was It joins the circle and the child who was chosen Señorita becomes It. The song is sung over again.

Cream - y rice pud-ding, I'm want-ing to wed With
Ar - roz con le - che, Me quie - ro ca - sar Con

a love-ly young la-dy From St. Nicholas. Is't this one? Yes? Is't
u - na se - ño - ri - ta De San Ni-co-las. Con és - ta? Sí? Con

this one? No! This is the love-ly la - dy I'm go -ing to wed.
és - ta? No! Con és-ta se - ño - ri - ta Me ca - se yo.

Variations of Arroz con Leche

The action is the same, but the words of the songs are different.

| *First version* | *Second version* |

Good white rice pudding,   I'm the young widower (widow)
I'm wanting to wed   From Big Moose Head;
A lovely señorita   I don't know who the girl (boy)
From Big Moose Head.   is
                               That I want to wed!

I hope she can sew,
Embroider well, too,   The one in red (blue, green, etc.)?
And play the games we   The little towhead?
    all like;   This lovely señorita
If so, she'll do!   I'm going to wed.

On the last stanza of this second version, the child in the center advances toward those in the circle, touches one of them tentatively at "The one in red" and then back again to the first choice in the declaration of marriage intention. The child chosen then goes to the center, to begin the game all over again. Sometimes all four stanzas are sung as one single song.—*Mrs. Vera L. Stockwell, Buenos Aires, Argentina.*

FISHER MARTIN
(Martín Piscador)

8-20 players, usually girls, 8-12 years   *Indoors or out of doors*

The game resembles "London Bridge" in all ways except for the verse that is sung. Since the music used in Argentina is not available, the words of the verse may be sung to the well known "London Bridge" air.

LINE OF CHILDREN: Fisherman, will you let us pass?
PAIR FORMING BRIDGE: You may pass, you may pass.
LINE OF CHILDREN: Fisherman, will you let us pass?
PAIR FORMING BRIDGE: The last must sta-ay!

—Miss Muriel David, Buenos Aires, Argentina.

Bolivia

THROW THE BEANS
(Tirar Fríjoles)

Pairs of boys or girls   *Out of doors*

A hole about eight inches around and two inches deep is made in the ground near a wall. For the first round the players stand about three feet from the hole. They take turns throwing beans which are a little smaller in size than the scarlet runner bean. Each player has a bag of beans.

Two play at a time as a rule. The first round each player starts with the same number of beans, say 7 each. The first person throws the 7 beans and those that go into the hole he keeps. The next person throws, and those that are thrown into the hole he keeps. The one who got the most beans into the hole has first turn to flick the beans that have missed the hole, and when he misses getting the beans in the hole by flicking, the next person has his turn. All those he flicks in he keeps. This is done until the 14 beans have been claimed.

For the second round, the players move back another two feet and throw again, say 12 beans each this time, reclaiming the beans that have fallen into the hole as before. A third and even a fourth round each at a greater distance from the hole may take place, provided the players have any beans left. The winner is the one who has the most beans.—*Mrs. Johnson Turnbull, Cochabamba, Bolivia.*

JACKSTONES

4 or 5 girls   *Out of doors*

The game is played with one marble and five smooth stones about the size in diameter of a nickel. One set. is used among a group of four or five players. A smooth bit of earth or stone is chosen upon which to play. The first player takes the five stones into the curve of her right hand, turns the palm over and allows the stones to fall gently so that they are scattered upon the prepared ground. They are left in that position. Then the marble is tossed into the air; the hand picks up one stone and moves back quickly to pick up the marble. The stone is placed by itself and the rest of the stones are picked up one by one. The stones are then scattered again. This time two stones are picked up in time to have the marble caught also, and so on until at last the five stones are picked up together. If the player is not quick enough to pick up the stones and allows the marble to fall to the ground, or drops the stones, she must pass the set on to the next player.—*Mrs. Johnson Turnbull, Cochabamba, Bolivia.*

MARBLES
(Cachinas)

2 boys or girls   *Out of doors*

Usually two boys play together. They place one marble in the center of a ring about six inches in diameter. A boy standing about three feet away lifts his right leg until the knee is high enough for the hand to be held against it comfortably. The marble is placed between the thumb and the first finger and it is flicked at the marble that is in the ring. If the boy knocks the marble out of the ring, he scores a point. Then the next player takes his turn with his two marbles. Then each player takes his turn in contributing one marble to the ring and whoever knocks it out of the ring scores a point.—*Mrs. Johnson Turnbull, Cochabamba, Bolivia.*

CHOQUE

Bolivian children are fond of playing *Choque* (cho'kay). They use a stick with two prongs or fork to which they have tied a wooden ball by means of a string from two to three feet long. Holding the stick by its "handle," the ball is tossed into the air and caught on the prongs.

THIEVES AND GUARDS
(Pillos y Rondinos)

Out of doors   *Similar to Prisoners' Base*
8-20 players, boys or girls

Sides of an equal number are chosen. For the first game one side is chosen to be *pillos* (thieves) and the other side to be *rondinos* (guards). The *pillos* make two bases opposite each other, the distance between the bases depending upon how much playing ground is available. The best place to play this game is in a large open space. Half the *pillos* go to one base and the other half of the *pillos* go to the second base. The *pillos* are expected to keep changing from base to base and while doing so try to keep out of the way of the *rondinos* who are waiting anywhere between the bases to catch them and take them to prison (a convenient place chosen by the *rondinos*). Once a *pillo* leaves a base he cannot return to it to avoid capture, but must run on to the second base. When all the *pillos* have been caught, the *rondinos* take over the bases and become *pillos,* and those who were *pillos* take their turn at being *rondinos.*—*Mrs. Johnson Turnbull, Cochabamba, Bolivia.*

Brazil

SICK CAT
(Gato Doente)

Out of doors   *Similar to Touch Tag*
                  6-30 players, 6-10 years

One player is chosen to be the Cat, or *Gato*. The other children are scattered about the playing field. At a signal, the *Gato* chases the others. Each one he is able to touch becomes a "sick cat" and must hold the part touched with the left hand. The "sick cats" chase the untouched players who when caught become "sick cats" themselves. The one who escapes without being touched by any "sick cat" wins the game.—*Miss Bernice M. Cartwright, Rio de Janeiro, Brazil.*

MY LITTLE BOAT
(A Canoa Virou)

10-30 boys and girls, 6-10 years   *Out of doors*

The children stand in a circle, holding hands, facing the center. They walk around to the left, holding hands and singing the first verse of the song. One after another, the name of each child in the circle is inserted in the song. As the child's name is spoken, he turns quickly, so that he faces outward, his back to the center, and he joins hands again. The first verse is repeated over and over again, until all the players have turned around and are facing outward. Then the second verse is sung and this time the children turn inward again, as their names are spoken. The second verse proceeds in the same way until all of the players have been "rescued" and the circle is once more as it was in the beginning. The game may be played over again, if desired.—*Helen H. Moreland, from "The Elementary Teacher."*

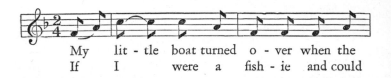

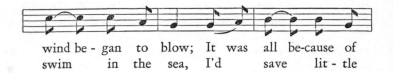

My lit-tle boat turned o-ver when the
If I were a fish-ie and could

wind be-gan to blow; It was all be-cause of
swim in the sea, I'd save lit-tle

Ma-ry, who had nev-er learned to row.
Ma-ry and take her home with me.

PETÉCA

Single player or many   *Out of doors*

The boys of Brazil like to play this game after school is over for the day. Their *petéca* is made in this way: They take a piece of leather, cut and sew it in the form of an empty cone. Then they fill it with sand. It is then about the size of a tennis ball. Into its open upper end they put several long feathers and tie them firmly.

The *petéca* is tossed into the air and kept there, each boy striking it upward with the palm of his hand. The players take turns, each hitting the *petéca,* only once at a time, and always upward. Often they repeat the letters of the alphabet as they play, one letter to each strike upward. If the *petéca* falls, the game must begin all over again.

In this country, children might use a badminton birdie for the game.—*Vera Andrade de Flores, Brazil*.

THE CHIEF ORDERS
(Chef Manda)

Indoors; a good party game   Similar to Do This, Do That
Many players, girls, 10-12 years

One player is the Chief. He stands in front of the others and gives orders which they must follow. For instance, when he says, "The Chief orders you to laugh," all the players must laugh. When he says, *"He* orders you to laugh," none of the children should laugh, because he did not say "the Chief." If a player does laugh or carry out any of the other orders beginning with "He" instead of "the Chief," he must get out of the game. The game proceeds until only one player is left besides the Chief and this player is the winner.—*Senhorita Elsy Ferreira, Colégio Americano, Pôrto Alegre, Brazil*.

DANCER, LITTLE DANCER
(Ciranda, Cirandenha)

Many players, boys and girls, 6-10 years   Indoors or out of doors

A circle is formed with the children holding hands and one child in the center. The children in the circle march to the left and sing the first part of the song. At the words "Let us turn," they change their direction and march to the right. At the end of the song the child who is in the center must repeat a poem, after which he takes his place in the circle.

Another child goes to the center and the song is repeated, the children tripping first to the left, then to the right.—*Senhorita Clelia de Aranjo, Colégio Americano, Pôrto Alegre, Brazil.*

Oh! Danc-er, lit-tle danc-er, Round a circ-le let us skip— Let us turn and dance a-gain— Round and half-way back, trip, trip.

THE CHICKEN FIGHT
(Luta de Galho)

2-20 players, usually girls, 10-14 years   *Out of doors*

Two players at a time engage each other and various teams may play at the same time. Each places a handkerchief in her belt and keeps her right arm folded across her breast. She hops about on her right foot. Her left foot may not touch the ground. With her free left arm she reaches for the handkerchief in the belt of her opponent, who may ward off the blows with her right elbow but may not unbend her arm. The play proceeds with each player bumping and pushing the other, and reaching for her opponent's handkerchief, while at the same time defending her own. The victor is the one who snatches her opponent's handkerchief in an unguarded moment. Any player whose left foot touches the ground or whose right arm unbends is disqualified. Sometimes the victor takes on the winner of another team and the play goes on until a final champion is proclaimed.—*B. M. Cartwright, Rio de Janeiro, Brazil.*

MY RIGHT SIDE IS VACANT
(Minha Direita Desocupada)

Indoors; a good party game   *Similar to Fruit Basket*
10 or more players

The players sit on chairs that form a circle, leaving one chair unoccupied. Each player chooses the name of a flower —rose, violet, pansy, and so on. The neighbor of the empty chair says, "My right side is vacant. Come here, Rose." The Rose gets up and takes the empty chair, leaving her last seat vacant. Her former neighbor must call some other flower to the empty chair and so the players go on changing places. If a player is called and pays no attention or forgets his name, he has to pay a forfeit.—*Senhorita Flavia Saint Pastores, Colégio Americano, Pôrto Alegre, Brazil.*

Chile

THE CAT AND THE MOUSE
(El Gato y el Ratón)

8-30 players, 5-10 years   *Indoors or out of doors*

The Cat and the Mouse are chosen first. The rest of the players form a circle holding hands. The Mouse will be inside the circle and the Cat outside. One of the players in the circle is assigned to be the Door. At the beginning of the game, the Cat knocks on the player who is the Door.

CAT: *¿Está la laucha?*	Is the mouse here?
DOOR: *Sí, se está lavando.*	Yes, but she is washing herself.

The Cat knows the Mouse is not ready (he is very polite), so he runs around the circle. He knocks again on the Door.

CAT: *¿Está la laucha?*	Is the mouse here?
DOOR: *Sí, se está peinando.*	Yes, but she is combing her hair.
CAT: *¿A qué horas saldrá?*	At what time will she be ready?
DOOR: *A las ocho.*	At eight o'clock.

Again the Cat goes around while all the players in the circle jump up and down eight times, as eight o'clock was the time mentioned. A third time the Cat comes to the Door.

CAT: *¿Está la laucha?*	Is the mouse here?
DOOR: *Sí, va saliendo.*	Yes, she is leaving.

Then the Cat may come into the circle and chase the Mouse. Both Cat and Mouse may run outside the circle, but the Cat has to pass through the same places that the Mouse has passed. The players in the circle have to raise their arms so that the Cat and Mouse can pass through. When the Mouse is caught, the Cat may become the Mouse and a new player is chosen for the Cat, or both Cat and Mouse may be changed. Some other player may be the Door also.—*Señorita Jenny Contesse, Chile.*

WHO IS IT?
(¿Quién Es?)

6-30 players, 6-14 years   *Indoors or out of doors*

The players form a line, one behind the other. The leader of the line is It and he begins the game by asking questions.

IT: *¿Han visto a mi amigo?*	Have you seen my friend?
OTHERS: *No, Señor.*	No, Sir.
IT: *¿Saben donde está?*	Do you know where he is?
OTHERS: *Sí Señor.*	Yes, Sir.

It takes nine slow steps forward, during which time the other players quickly change their places in the line in any way they wish. One of them takes his place directly behind It, who thus cannot see who is there. The other players begin to call *"¿Quién es?"* (Who is it?) It tries to guess who it is. He may ask three questions of the other players before he guesses, such as, *¿Es niña o niño?* (Is it girl or boy?) *¿Es alto o bajo?* (Is he tall or short?) *¿Es moreno o rubio?* (Is he dark or fair?) After he has asked these questions, he has to guess who stands behind him. If he guesses right, he has another turn. If he guesses wrong, another child becomes It. —*Señorita Jenny Contesse, Chile.*

THE HEN RUNS
(La Gallina Que Se Va)

Out of doors   *Similar to London Bridge*
8-20 players, girls, 6-12

The general directions for "London Bridge" may be followed for this game. Each girl in the arch selects a different name of a fruit, flower, or animal. The other players form a line by placing their hands on the hips of the player in front. They go running around the field in line and as they run, they repeat, "Pa! Pa! Pa! The hen runs." (*Pa! Pa! Pa! La gallina que se va.*) They run through the arch and pass through it, the last one in the line being caught. The line runs through again and again, repeating the same refrain until all have been caught and have chosen sides. The game ends in a tug of war.—*Señorita Jenny Contesse, Chile.*

THE SEA IS ROUGH
(El Mar Está Agitado)

Indoors or out of doors   *Similar to Fruit Basket*
8-30 players, 8-12 years

One player is chosen to be It. The other players sit in a circle with their legs crossed. Each player marks a cross on the ground in front of him. It stands in the center of the circle and gives to each player the name of a fish. After this he moves around the outside of the circle, saying, "The sea is very rough today. Let the swordfish (for example) come out." The player who has that name leaves his place and begins to run outside the circle after the one who is It. As he runs, It keeps calling the names of fish that he gave to the different players. As soon as a player is called, he must leave his place and run around the circle with the others. As soon as It has some six players running after him, he says, "The sea is rough. Let all the fish come out." All the rest of the players get up and run around the circle after It.

After two or three turns, It says, "The sea is calm now." Then each player tries to get back to his original place in the circle as quickly as possible. It may sit in any place that is free. The player who cannot find a place becomes the new It.—*Señorita Jenny Contesse, Chile.*

Colombia

THE RING ON THE STRING
(El Anillo en la Cuerda)

For parties and fiestas   *Similar to Pass the Ring*
8-20 players, children and adults

One person is chosen to be It and stands inside a circle made by the players standing or sitting very close together. A long string and a ring to slip along it are provided. The string must be long enough so that when both ends are tied, it makes a circle of the same size as the one formed by the children.

Each child grasps the string in front of him with both hands, holding it loosely, so that the ring can travel easily along the string from player to player. Each player moves his hands along the string from the sides to the center, where both then meet and separate again. When separated, they meet the hands of the players at the right and left sides. This movement of the hands is continuous throughout the game, and by means of it the ring is passed from hand to hand around the circle along the string. Often the player will be unaware of the location of the ring until he suddenly feels it placed in his hand by a neighbor.

As the game starts, the players begin to sing:

> The prize is in the hand,
> The prize is in the hand,
> It passed by here
> And it left me a flower.

The ring passes along the string and It watches to see if he can locate where it is. He catches the hand that he supposes is holding the ring and he shouts, "Here it is!"

Many times the children get so busy trying to receive and pass on the ring that they may forget to continue singing. Instead of the song, false movements of the hands and jeering to confuse the guesser are very frequent. The ring starts moving around the circle in one direction. If the players are skillful they may make it go in the opposite direction.

If the ring is in the hand that It selects, the player who holds it goes to the center of the circle. It takes his place. In case It guesses wrong, he has to try again. When he has failed several times, he is usually replaced by a volunteer.— *Señorita Isabel Giraldo, Colombia.*

LITTLE GREEN STICK
(Palito Verde)

Indoors or out of doors   *Similar to Drop the Handkerchief*
8-20 players, 8-12 years

A little green branch is chosen to be dropped upon the ground, though other objects, particularly handkerchiefs, are often used. One child is chosen to be It and he carries the green branch. The other players form a circle, holding hands, and say, *"¿Palito verde?"* (Pah-lee'toh ver'deh, meaning "What is the little green stick?") to It who is walking around outside the circle. It replies, *"Romero"* (roe-mer'o), which means "rosemary." The chorus and answer are repeated a number of times, with the object of giving the moving child opportunity to pass behind all of the children. When It has completed the circle, the chorus ceases its call. It begins to run around the circle, repeating, "There it is; there it is." He drops the green stick behind a child who is not watching him. As soon as the child notices the stick behind him, he quickly picks it up and chases It, who must run around the complete circle until he reaches the place left vacant by his pursuer. If he is touched by the stick before he reaches his goal, he must be It once more. If he reaches his goal safely, the child now holding the stick must be It.—*Señorita Isabel Giraldo, Colombia.*

Peru

WOLF, ARE YOU READY?
(¿Lobo, Ya Estás?)

6-20 players, 8-12 years   *Out of Doors*

One of the players is chosen to be the Wolf and he hides. The rest of the players hold hands, forming a circle. They dance around the place where the Wolf is hiding. As they dance, they sing or call out,

> While the wolf gets ready
> Let us play in the woods.
> Are you ready, Wolf, are you ready?

The wolf replies, "I am just getting up."

The children continue to dance and repeat the same song with its question, "Are you ready?" The Wolf each time gives answer, "I am putting on my pants," "I am putting on my shirt," "I am putting on my coat," "I am putting on my hat." The Wolf may add various articles of clothing until at last he shouts loudly, "I am *ready!*" He dashes out of his hiding place after the players, who all start to run away at his shout. The one he catches will be the Wolf for the next game.—*Señora Wenceslao Bahamonde, Lima, Peru.*

THE CLOCK
(El Reloj)

4-20 players   *Out of doors*

This is a jumping-rope game. Two players hold the ends of a big rope so they can swing it high. The other players stand one behind the other. The object of this game is to give the hour by the number of steps the player jumps in the swinging rope. The first player marks zero by running through the swinging rope without jumping or being touched. The next runs in, jumps once and runs out. The next follows immediately, jumping twice and running out. The jumping continues in this way until twelve is reached. If a player misses or is touched by the rope, he changes places with one of the children who is swinging the rope and the game starts again. The game should be played at a fast rate.—*Señora Wenceslao Bahamonde, Lima, Peru.*

THE KING MAY PASS
(Que Pase el Rey)

Indoors or out of doors   *Similar to London Bridge*
8-20 players, 6-12 years

This game is one of the variations of "London Bridge," and the general directions given for "The Fountain" on page 89 may be followed. In this variation the children hold on to each other. They sing this little song as they run under the arch.

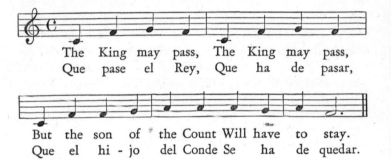

The   King   may   pass,   The   King   may   pass,
Que   pase   el   Rey,   Que   ha   de   pasar,

But   the   son   of   the Count   Will   have   to   stay.
Que   el   hi - jo   del Conde   Se   ha   de   quedar.

The two players who form the arch choose secret names for themselves, such as the Sun and the Moon. When all the players have been caught and made their choice of belonging to the Sun or Moon, a tug of war is held to the end of the game.—*Señora Wenceslao Bahamonde, Lima, Peru.*

AMPAY

Out of doors   *Similar to Hide and Seek*
8-20 players, 7-14 years

An empty can with a few pebbles in it is needed for the game. One player is chosen to be It. Another player throws the can as far as he is able. It must go and pick up the can, and carry it to a goal which has been chosen beforehand. While he is doing this, the rest of the players hide in different places near by. All players should be hidden by the time It has laid the can at goal. Immediately he tries to find the other players. If he sees anybody from goal, he cries out, "Ampay," and names the player and place where he is. (For example, "Ampay! Mary, behind the bench.") And he shakes the can with the pebbles. Then Mary is out of the game. If he does not see any others, he has to leave the goal and look for them. Every time he catches sight of one, he must run to goal to shake the can and call out the name of the person and where he is, thus putting that player out. He continues in this way until he has found and put out all the players. If, when he is looking for a player, another one can reach the can and shake it without being seen, he saves all the others, as he shouts, "Ampay! Everybody saved!" If all have been saved, the same player must be It again. If not, the first one found and called becomes the next It.—*Señora Wenceslao Bahamonde, Lima, Peru.*

Games of America North of Mexico

THE games played by the majority of the children in the part of America that lies north of Mexico were brought, in the first place, by people who came from many different lands. The children who came to America played the games they had learned in their homelands. They taught them to their playmates and learned from them many games that were fresh and new. As a result, the children of North America know and play a great variety of games. Some of these games have maintained their original form, but over the years many have become so changed and adapted that it is hard to tell from which country they originally came. In addition, new ones have been invented. A number of new and adapted games are included in this section.

Descriptions of games played by the different national groups who have come to North America will be found listed under the country of origin, except for such groups as the French Canadians, the Negroes, the Spanish Americans, and the Southern Mountaineers, whose games are so individual that some typical ones have been introduced in this section.

Of course, the Indian and Eskimo children were playing games before the white men came. They are still playing their own games, though they have learned new ones as well. A number of their games are given under the geographical divisions of Alaska, Canada, and the United States. As you might expect, the children who live in the towns and cities of Alaska play the same games as do boys and girls in the United States, or in the countries from which their parents may have come.

ALASKA

The original inhabitants of Alaska, the Eskimos and the Tlingit Indians, have games of their own, taught to them by their parents and their comrades. Though many of them now play other games as well, they still enjoy their own.

Eskimo

MUSK OXEN

6-20 players, 7-10 years   *Out of doors*

Eskimo boys like to play at hunting musk oxen. One of them pulls the skin of a musk ox over his head. He runs and dodges about while the other boys circle around and try to hit him with blunt arrows. If you want to play this game, you might use a blanket for an ox skin and blunt sticks for arrows.

A variation of this game is played by choosing two children to be It. They approach the other children, and as soon as they call, "Musk Ox," the others chase them. If they are tagged before reaching the base they have chosen, the taggers become It.—*From "Alaskan Play Hour," by Katharine E. Gladfelter.*

FOOTBALL

8-20 players, 8-16 years   *Out of doors*

The game is usually played in the winter, often on the hard, drifted snow, though it may be played along the ground in the spring. A ball made of leather, stuffed with deer hair or moss, is used (a basketball or volleyball may be substituted). Two leaders are chosen and each one chooses a player alternately until all are divided. Some twenty yards apart, two conspicuous parallel marks are made on the snow or ground. These serve as goals. The players of each side stand along their goal line. The ball is tossed upon the ground midway between them. The players rush at the ball. Each side tries to drive the ball by kicks and blows across the goal line of the opposing team.—*From "The Eskimo about Bering Strait."*

FOLLOW THE LEADER

3-25 players, boys and girls   *Out of doors*

One child is chosen to be the leader and the others follow after him. The game is played on the snow, often just after a fresh fall. The leader runs along the snow, taking different kinds of steps. He may turn his toes inward or outward, jump forward with both feet, hop first on one foot and then on the other. All the children following him must do just as he does.

CATCH THE BAG

4-20 players, 8-12 years   *Indoors or out of doors*

The Eskimo boys and girls play a game with something that looks like a beanbag but is made of sealskin and filled with sand. The players stand in a circle and toss the bag from one to another. Anyone who fails to catch the bag when it is thrown to him must leave the circle. The last player in the circle wins the game.

Tlingit Indians of Southeastern Alaska

GUESSING GAME

3-20 players, 8-12 years   *Indoors or out of doors*

One child is chosen to be It and he is given twenty or more small sticks. The other children close their eyes tightly and It arranges the sticks in a series of groups on the ground. When

It calls "Ready" the other players shout out their guesses as to the number of groups of sticks on the ground. The one who first guesses the correct number of groups becomes the next It.
—*From "Alaskan Play Hour," by Katharine E. Gladfelter.*

COME HERE
(Hagoo)

10-30 players, 8 years and up   *Indoors or out of doors*

The players are divided into two groups, one made up of boys and one of girls. Older people also take delight in this game, which is enjoyed by all ages. Each side chooses a captain.

If the girls have the first turn, they will decide on the name of some boy in the other line. The girls form a double line, at the head of which the captain stands on a chair or box, holding a handkerchief or cloth in her hand. The captain waves the handkerchief or cloth and all the girls call, *"Hagoo,* John," or whatever name has been chosen. This boy must walk between the double line of girls without smiling and get the cloth away from the leader, who will hold it beyond his reach so that he must jump for it. The girls try their best to make him smile. A continual calling of *"Hagoo,* John," is kept up until he gets the cloth and returns with it along the double line without breaking into a smile. If he succeeds, his side greets him with cheers. If he smiles before obtaining the handkerchief, he is held a prisoner until some other boy is able to pass the test. Often there will be several players held captive before the hand-kerchief can be taken to the other side.

Then it is the turn of the boys, who will call out *"Hagoo,* Mary," or whatever name is chosen, and the same procedure is carried out. It adds much to the amusement of the game when a person is called who is known to have difficulty in keeping a straight face. There seems to be no set time when the game ends. The players enjoy it so much that the calling back and forth is kept up indefinitely.—*Miss Emily Sidebotham, Sheldon Jackson School, Sitka, Alaska.*

CANADA

The boys and girls of Canada play many of the same games as do the children of the United States. Many of their games had their origin in Europe, from which came most of the racial groups that make up the population. A few of the common games have been included with their variations. Descriptions of two games played by the Huron Indians of Ontario have been given as they were noted by Father Hennepin. These two games are typical of those played by many Indian tribes.

PASS THE BROOM

10-30 players, 6-12 years   *Indoors*

The children form a fairly large circle, facing inwards. Each player puts one hand behind his back. A broom is passed from one player to another, while music is played on piano or phonograph. When the music stops, the child who is holding the broom must drop from the circle. The last to remain in the circle is the winner.—*Miss Ella Des Brisay, Halifax, Canada.*

HIDE THE PENCIL

5-20 players, 6-10 years   *Indoors*

All the children but one leave the room. The child who is left hides a pencil where it can be plainly seen. The other children are called back and are told that the pencil is in plain sight and nothing needs to be moved or touched to see it.

As each child sees the pencil, he goes and sits down quietly.

The hunt continues until all have discovered the hiding place of the pencil. The one who was first to see it has the next chance to hide it, while the others go out of the room.—*Miss Ella Des Brisay, Halifax, Canada.*

TANUARY

Out of doors   *Similar to Pom, Pom, Pullaway*
                 6-20 players, 10-12 years

One player is chosen to be It. The following counting out rhyme may be used:

> Wonery, orery, ickery, Ann,
> Fillacy, fallacy, Nicholas John,
> Queever, quover, Irish Mary,
> Stinkalum, stankalum, bee, bo, buck.

A section of a quiet street may be the playing ground, with the sidewalks representing the two safety zones. Or a part of a playground may be marked off with a space for running, with safety zones at each end.

It stands midway between the two safety zones and the other players are drawn up along the safety line facing him. One by one they begin to run across to the other safety zone, It chasing them and trying to catch them. If the players do not run fast enough to suit him, It calls out:

> Tanuary, Tanuary, one, two, three,
> If you don't run now,
> I'll catch you where you be.

Everyone must then run across to the other side.

Whenever a player is caught, he stays with It and becomes a pursuer. After a time there is likely to be only one child on a safety line while all the others are trying to catch him. He must run if the Tanuary rhyme is used. When he is caught, the game is ended; but it usually begins again with the first one caught as It.—*Miss Edith M. Creighton, Halifax, Canada.*

HERE COMES A KNIGHT A-RIDING

6-20 players, usually girls, 8-10 years   *Indoors or out of doors*

One child is chosen to be the Knight and the others are Maidens who form a line in front of the Knight and about six or eight feet from him. The Knight and the Maidens sing alternate verses of the song. Whichever side is singing advances on the words of the song and retreats on the refrain.

Here comes a Knight a - rid - ing, For the
And wh - at do you come for, For the

Ran - cy Tan - cy Tis - sa - bye - o. Here
Ran - cy Tan - cy Tis - sa - bye - o? And

comes a Knight a - rid - ing, For the
wha - at do you come for, For the

Ran - cy Tan - cy Tee.
Ran - cy Tan - cy Tee?

KNIGHT: I've come to get a maiden, etc.
MAIDENS: And which one will you have, sir? etc.
KNIGHT: You're all too black and dirty, etc.
MAIDENS: We're just as good as you are, etc.
KNIGHT: I think I will have this one, etc.

The Knight indicates one of the Maidens, who crosses over to him and then becomes a Knight. The verses are sung over again, this time beginning with "Here come two Knights a-riding." The game proceeds until all the Maidens have become Knights.—*Miss Nina Millen, Toronto, Canada, and New York City.*

HIDE THE BELL

Children, 5-8 years   *Indoors*

One child is chosen to be It and he goes out of the room. The other children are asked to hide their hands or to put them in their desks (if they are in the classroom). A small bell is given to one of the children. It is called back into the room. The bell tinkles and It has to guess from the sound who has the bell. If he guesses correctly, the child who had it goes out of the room. The bell is given to another and the game continues. Very small children may be given three chances at guessing.—*Originated in classroom of Miss Ella Des Brisay, Halifax, Canada.*

OLD ROGER

8-20 players, 6-12 years   *Indoors or out of doors*

The children form a circle and two players are chosen to be Old Roger and the Old Woman. The children stand and sing the following song, while Old Roger and the Old Woman act out the words of the song.

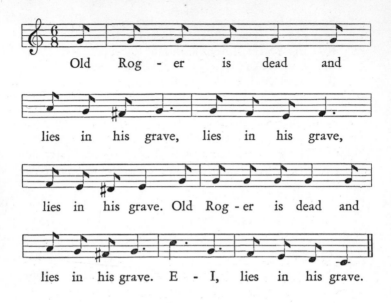

Old Rog - er   is   dead   and

lies   in   his   grave,   lies   in   his   grave,

lies   in   his   grave. Old Rog - er   is   dead   and

lies   in   his   grave.   E - I,   lies   in   his   grave.

While the first verse is being sung, Old Roger lies on the ground, making believe he is dead. The Old Woman remains inside the circle.

> They planted an apple tree over his head,
> Over his head, over his head.
> They planted an apple tree over his head,
> E-I, over his head.

Children all raise arms over their heads with palms pointing downward toward Old Roger.

> The apples got ripe and all tumbled down,
> All tumbled down, all tumbled down.
> The apples got ripe and all tumbled down,
> E-I, all tumbled down.

Hands and arms are lowered to music to represent apples falling.

> There came an Old Woman, a-picking them up,
> A-picking them up, a-picking them up.
> There came an Old Woman, a-picking them up,
> E-I, a-picking them up.

The Old Woman comes into the circle and stoops as though she were picking up apples and dropping them into her apron.

> Old Roger got up and gave her a thump,
> Gave her a thump, gave her a thump.
> Old Roger got up and gave her a thump,
> E-I, gave her a thump.

Old Roger comes to life and follows the Old Woman about inside the circle, thumping her to the words of the music.

> This made the Old Woman go hippety-hop,
> Hippety-hop, hippety-hop.
> This made the Old Woman go hippety-hop,
> E-I, hippety-hop.

The Old Woman hobbles about with a limp, bent over with one hand on the knee.—*Miss Ella Des Brisay, Halifax, Canada.*

HOIST YOUR SAILS

10-30 players, 10-14 years   *Out of doors*

Two captains are chosen, usually the natural leaders in the group. The captains choose sides and the decision is made as to who will have the first chance at hiding.

One side takes a treasure, which may be almost anything from a boy's pocket, and they go off to hide it. They return to where the other side is waiting. With a stick the captain draws on the ground a map showing where the treasure is hidden. The other team goes in search of the treasure. The team may have to return to refer to the map several times, but once the treasure is found they come back and hoist a sail (a stick with a handkerchief tied to it will serve). They now take the treasure and hide it, coming back to draw a map that will show where it is to be found.—*Miss Ella Des Brisay, Halifax, Canada.*

DROP THE HANDKERCHIEF

10-30 players, 6-12 years   *Indoors or out of doors*

The children form a circle, standing about two feet apart. The child chosen to be It walks and then runs around the outside of the circle with a handkerchief in his hand, which he drops behind a standing player, trying to select one who seems to be inattentive. The player must stoop, pick up the handkerchief, and chase It, trying to touch him before he gets all around the circle and into the place that has been left vacant. If It is caught, he must carry the handkerchief again. If he is not caught, the other player becomes It.

In Canada the children sing a verse to the tune of "Yankee Doodle" as It moves around the circle. All join in the song.

> I wrote a letter to my love,
> And on the way I dropped it.
> A little puppy picked it up,
> And put it in his pocket.
>
> I won't bite you, I won't bite you, etc., etc.,
> But I *will* bite you.

The last two lines are chanted by It, who begins to run as fast as he can as soon as he has said, "I will bite you."—*Miss Nina Millen, Toronto, Canada, and New York City.*

French Canadian Games

PLANTING CABBAGE
(Savez-vous Planter des Choux?)

6-20 players, 5-8 years   *Indoors or out of doors*

The children form a single circle facing toward the center.
They join hands and move to the right as they sing verse one.

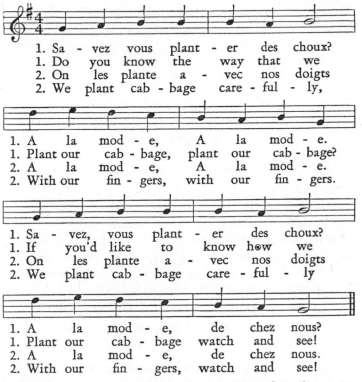

1. Sa - vez vous plant - er des choux?
1. Do you know the way that we
2. On les plante a - vec nos doigts
2. We plant cab - bage care - ful - ly,

1. A la mod - e, A la mod - e.
1. Plant our cab - bage, plant our cab - bage?
2. A la mod - e, A la mod - e.
2. With our fin - gers, with our fin - gers.

1. Sa - vez, vous plant - er des choux?
1. If you'd like to know how we
2. On les plante a - vec nos doigts
2. We plant cab - bage care - ful - ly

1. A la mod - e, de chez nous?
1. Plant our cab - bage watch and see!
2. A la mod - e, de chez nous.
2. With our fin - gers, watch and see!

At verse two, the children stop moving, face the center,
make the motions of digging earth with their fingers, and

pretend to put cabbage plants in the ground. At verse three, the children face the center and make motions of patting the earth with their feet. At verse four, they face center and move their elbows up and down. At verse five they face center and nod their heads. Between each verse they join hands, move in a circle, and sing the words of verse one.

In the French version, *"avec nos doigts"* in verse two becomes *"avec nos pieds"* in verse three, *"avec nos coudes"* in verse four, and *"avec nos têtes"* in verse five.

In the English version, "with our fingers," in verse two becomes "with our two feet" in verse three, "with our elbows" in verse four, and "with our heads" in verse five.—*Misses Dorothy Leslie and Anne Hawkins, Scarboro Bluffs, Canada.*

ON THE BRIDGE OF AVIGNON
(Sur le Pont d'Avignon)

8-25 players, boys and girls, 6-10 years   Indoors or out of doors

The children join hands and dance in a circle while they sing the first part of each verse of the song. On the last line of each verse they stand still and act out the words.

On the last line of the first verse, the children all bow from their waists, first holding their right arms bent in front of their waists and their left arms straight out, and then their left arms in front and their right arms straight out.

Sur le pont d' Avignon, l'on y danse, l'on y danse;
Sur le pont d' Avignon, l'on y danse, tout en rond.
Les beaux messieurs font comme ci, et puis encore comme ça.

In the French version only a few words are changed for the various verses. *"Les beaux messieurs"* of verse one becomes *"Les belles dames"* for verse two; *"Les soldats"* for verse three;

"*Les blanchiseuses*" for verse four; "*Les cordonniers*" for verse five; and "*Les abbés*" for verse six. Appropriate actions are made to accompany each verse.

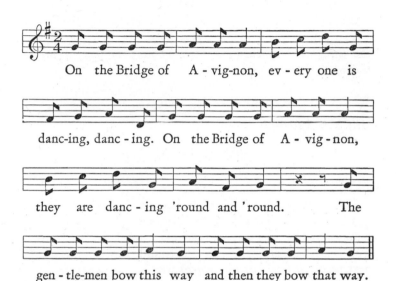

On the Bridge of A - vig-non, ev - ery one is danc-ing, danc - ing. On the Bridge of A - vig-non, they are danc - ing 'round and 'round. The gen - tle-men bow this way and then they bow that way.

In the English version the last line of the song changes from verse to verse. The action suggested by the words is carried out by the children as they sing.

> The ladies curtsy this way,
> And then curtsy that way.

> The soldiers salute this way,
> And then salute that way.

> The washwomen scrub this way,
> And then they scrub that way.

The shoemakers tap this way,
And then they tap that way.

The abbots fold hands this way,
And then fold them that way.

On the sixth verse the children fold their hands piously.

The game ends with the repeating of the first two lines of the song as a conclusion.—*Miss Yvonne Gignac, Windsor, Canada.*

Indian Games

GUESS HOW MANY

2-12 players   *Indoors or out of doors*

The children use kernels of Indian corn or pebbles for this game. One child hides the kernels in one of his hands. "Guess how many" he says to one child after another in the group. The child who guesses the correct number wins and has the next turn.—*From "Writings of Father Louis Hennepin."*

TIPCAT

2-12 players, usually boys, 8-14 years   *Out of doors*

The game is played with two sticks, one large and one small. The child who is the batter holds the small stick in the left hand and the large stick in the right. The small stick is tossed into the air and then struck with the large one. The other children run after the small stick. The one who gets it throws it at the batter, and if he touches him, he wins the next turn to bat. If he misses, the batter has another turn.—*From "Writings of Father Louis Hennepin."*

UNITED STATES

From the hundreds of games played by children in the United States, only a few representative ones could be included in this book. Some are old games; some are new; some came from other lands; and some have been adapted by use in this country. The games played in the Southern Mountain section where the people have been isolated have changed little since they were brought from England long ago. The Negro and Spanish American children have games that they especially enjoy, and a few are given in this section.

BUM, BUM, HERE WE COME

20-30 players, boys and girls   *Out of doors*

The players are divided into two sides. They draw lines about ten feet apart and each side stands along one of the lines. The side that has first turn confers as to what work they are going to act out in pantomime, such as picking flowers, washing or ironing clothes, picking apples, rowing a boat, and so forth. When they have made their decision, they advance a few feet in a line towards the opposite side, chanting, "Bum, bum, here we come!"

The other line advances a few feet and asks, "Where are you from?"

The dialogue follows:

FIRST SIDE: Pennsylvania.

SECOND SIDE: What's your trade?

FIRST SIDE: Lemonade.

SECOND SIDE: Then show us what you're doing, if you're not afraid.

Then the side that is going to pantomime begins to act out

picking of flowers, washing or ironing of clothes, picking of apples, or whatever else has been chosen.

The other side must guess what the actors are doing. Upon guessing correctly, they chase the players of the opposite side. Those caught before they pass their home goal line go to the other side. The game proceeds with that side being allowed to choose a pantomime. The game proceeds until all the players are caught and remain on one side.—*Miss Anne Shannon, Poteau, Oklahoma, and New York City.*

GRUNT, PIG, GRUNT

8-20 players, 6-12 years   *Indoors or out of doors*

The players stand in a circle and the one chosen to be It is placed in the center. It is blindfolded and given a long stick (a yardstick will do). It is turned about several times. Then he goes toward the outer circle, holding his pointer before him. When the pointer touches a player in the circle, It says, "Grunt, pig, grunt." The person who is thus spoken to grunts, and It tries to guess the identity of the player. It may touch the player three times and ask him to grunt while It tries to identify the voice. If he guesses correctly, the grunter becomes the next It and the old It joins the circle. If he fails to identify the person, he has to try again.—*Miss Edith Welker, Hartford, Connecticut.*

ARCHES

12-36 players, 6-9 years   *Indoors*

The children form a circle. Two of them form an arch by facing each other and holding their upraised hands. The remaining players march to music through the arch in circle formation. When the music stops, the two players forming the arch try to catch the person marching through it. As soon as two players have been caught, they form a second arch at a different spot in the circle. When two more are caught, they form a third arch at still another spot in the circle and so on until one player is left. That one is the winner of the game. If music is not available, the game may be played with a whistle. At the sound of the whistle, the "arch" players try to catch the one marching under their arms. To keep the game interesting and active, short and irregular steps are best with no running allowed.—*Miss Bligh Des Brisay, Great Neck, N. Y.*

GOING TO JERUSALEM

10-40 players, 9-16 years   *Indoors*

One player is chosen to be It and all the others get chairs for themselves, which they place in a long line, one chair facing right, the chair next it facing left, and so on down the line. There is one less chair than players, It having no seat.

The leader should be seated at the piano or have a whistle.

It has a cane or yardstick and he starts walking around the line of chairs in which the players are seated. He chants, "I am going to Jerusalem! I am going to Jerusalem!" He stops now and then to knock on a chair with his cane. This is the signal for the one seated in the chair to get up and follow him. Sometimes the player called has to run around the line of chairs to get behind It. The next player called follows behind him and so on until all are marching around the chairs in a single line with It at the head. It may turn and move in the opposite direction if he desires, and all the players have to follow him.

Music may have been playing softly all this time and when it stops or when the whistle blows, the players, including It, make a scramble for the chairs. The player who is left without a chair must drop out of the game. In case two players contend for a chair, the one who covers most of the seat wins.

The player who is out must take a chair off the end of the line and carry it to the side, where he may sit watching the game. The player who was seated on it becomes the next It, moving around the line with the cane as he chants, "I am going to Jerusalem!" The game continues until there are two players and one chair left. The one who first seats himself on the chair when the music stops or the whistle blows wins the game.

WHICH AM I?

6-15 players, 5-9 years   *Indoors or out of doors*

The group stands in a circle. One is chosen to stand in the center. This person is blindfolded or closes his eyes tightly. Those in the outer circle say, "Now I am very, very tall (players on toes—arms straight up), now I am very, very small (players in stooping position), very tall, very small— now which am I?" While the words are being repeated, the appropriate action is given. On the words, "Now which am I?" the group takes either an upright or stooping position. The person in the center tries to tell by locating the voices which position has been taken by the group. If the guess is correct, a new center is chosen. If incorrect, another guess is made.—*Miss Edith Welker, Hartford, Connecticut.*

FRUIT BASKET

10-30 players   *Indoors or out of doors*

All of the players except the one who is It are seated in a circle. It stands within the circle and gives the name of a fruit to each player. If the group is large, some of the names may be duplicated. A narrator, the leader, or occasionally It, if the players are older children, tells a story, being sure to bring into it the names of fruits in groups of two or more. For example,

"When I was walking in the country, I saw some beautiful *apples* and *cherries*." Immediately the players who were named for those fruits exchange places, while It tries to get into one of the vacant spots left in the circle before the exchange is completed. If he succeeds, the player who is left without a place becomes It. If he fails, he is It for another turn. When the words "fruit basket" are brought into the story, all players must exchange places.—*Miss Bligh Des Brisay, Great Neck, N. Y.*

BAT THE BALLOON

10-30 players, 6-10 years   *Indoors or out of doors*

The players are divided into two teams, which sit on the floor in two lines, facing each other. Each player has his legs extended so that the soles of his feet touch the soles of the opposite player. The left hand of each player is placed behind his back and is not used in the game. A ballon is thrown into the center of the lines by the leader. The players bat it with their right hands as it comes within their reach. When one team succeeds in batting it over the heads of its opponents so that it lands on the floor behind, a point is scored for that team. The balloon is tossed into the center again and the play continues. The team gaining the most points wins.—*Miss Bligh Des Brisay, Great Neck, N. Y.*

JUMP THE BEANBAG

10-40 players, 8-14 years   *Indoors or out of doors*

This is a rather noisy, active game, but it is a popular one. A small beanbag is tied on the end of a rope or heavy cord. The leader stands in the center of a circle made up of the players who are facing inward and standing about arm's length apart. The distance of the circle from the leader should be the length of the beanbag rope. It leans over and swings the beanbag around the circle at ankle height. Each player jumps over the bag as it approaches him. If a player is struck by the bag, he must leave the circle. The last player, the one who succeeds in jumping the bag for the longest time, is the winner. Any player who is hit above the knees by the bag is not disqualified, as the bag should be swung low.—*Miss Bligh Des Brisay, Great Neck, N. Y.*

HE CAN DO LITTLE

8-20 players, 9-15 years   *Indoors*

The players are seated in a circle. One player who knows the "secret" has a yardstick or other similar stick. Tapping it on the floor in rhythm to the words he repeats, "He can do little who can't do this." The stick is passed to the next player who tries to copy the action and words exactly. The trick is that the first player passed the stick from his *right* to his *left* hand and then on to the second player. The play continues until a number of players can discover the trick and imitate the action.—*Miss Edith Welker, Hartford, Connecticut.*

Negro Game

SEA LION

7-39 players, boys and girls, 10 years and up   *Indoors or out of doors*

There should be an uneven number of players. One player is the leader and stands in the center and chants the verses. The others divide into pairs and form a single circle, with the partners standing next to each other. All the players in the circle clap hands as the verses are sung and the entire group joins in the refrain of "Sea Lion" all through the song.

The leader skips around the circle and takes somebody else's partner. The two of them skip around in the middle of the circle for as long a time as they wish. Then they skip to the circle and take their place there. The player who has been left without a partner becomes the new leader. He skips around the circle and chooses a partner, and the action is repeated.

If there are many players, there may be a number of Its and several couples skipping in the circle at the same time. The chorus and first verse are included with the music. The other verses are given below. The chorus should be repeated after each verse.

Chorus: Hey, hey, hey! Sea Lion! Won't
Way down yon - der, Sea Lion! A -

you be mine? Sea Lion! You won't do nothin',
bout the sun, Sea Lion! My moth - er called me,

Sea Lion! But starch and iron. Sea Lion!
Sea Lion! A su - gar plum. Sea Lion!

Old rabbit hip. Sea Lion! Old rabbit hop. Sea Lion!
Old rabbit bit. Sea Lion! My turnip top. Sea Lion!

If I live. Sea Lion! To get twenty-one. Sea Lion!
I'm going to marry. Sea Lion! Somebody's son. Sea Lion!

See that man. Sea Lion! With the blue shirt on. Sea Lion!
You'd better leave. Sea Lion! That man alone. Sea Lion!

—*Words set down by Miss Thelma Moore and Miss Christine Steward; music by Mrs. Gertrude Smith Jackson, Southern Christian Institute, Edwards, Mississippi.*

Southern Mountain Games

HERE WE GO OVER THE MOUNTAIN
TWO BY TWO

14-50 players, 6-10 years   *Indoors or out of doors*

Partners are chosen and the children march counterclockwise in a double circle. One couple is chosen to stand in the center of the circle. Those in the double circle march singing the first stanza:

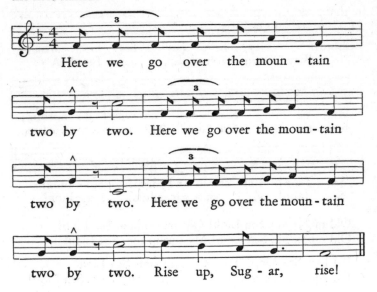

Here we go over the moun - tain
two by two. Here we go over the moun - tain
two by two. Here we go over the moun - tain
two by two. Rise up, Sug - ar, rise!

During the singing of this stanza, the two in the center determine upon some action that they can carry out together. At the beginning of the second stanza while the children still march about, the two in the center carry out the action they have chosen as those marching sing:

> Show us a pretty motion, two by two,
> Show us a pretty motion, two by two,
> Show us a pretty motion, two by two,
>   Rise up, Sugar, rise.

As the entire group sings the third stanza,

> Very pretty motion, two by two,
> Very pretty motion, two by two,
> Very pretty motion, two by two,
>   Rise up, Sugar, rise.

Each couple acts out the motion that has been demonstrated by those in the center. At the end of the stanza, the two in the center choose another couple to take their place and the game continues.

The action should be such as can be carried out by two persons, such as pretending to throw a ball to each other, linking arms and twirling, joining hands and skipping, some simple form of bean porridge hot, or any other action that will bring both players into the game.—*Miss Edith Welker, Hartford, Connecticut.*

SHEEP-NANNY

6-20 players, 9-12 years   *Indoors or out of doors*

One player is the Leader and the rest are Sheep.

The Leader calls to her Sheep, "She-e-ep-nanny! She-e-ep-nanny! She-e-ep-nanny!"

The sheep follow in a bunch behind the Leader calling, "Ba-a-a-a!"

The Leader turns quickly and tries to tag the Sheep. They run for safety to a circle that has been previously marked out on the ground or floor. The Leader tries to pull the Sheep out of the circle, one at a time. She may step one foot but not both feet over the line of the circle as she pulls at the Sheep. Each

Sheep pulled out helps the Leader pull the others. Those inside try to pull the outer ones back. The game is over when all the Sheep are pulled out or the Leader and all the Sheep are pulled in.—*As played at Williams' Branch, Perry County, Kentucky. From "Circle Left."*

BLUEBIRD, BLUEBIRD

8-20 players, usually girls, 6-10 years   *Indoors or out of doors*

1. Blue - bird, blue - bird through my   win - dow,
2. Take a little girl   and   pat her on the shoulder,

1. Blue - bird, blue - bird through my   win - dow,
2. Take a little girl   and   pat   her on the shoulder,

1. Blue - bird, blue - bird through my   win - dow,
2. Take a little girl   and   pat   her on the shoulder,

1. Ho!   John - ny   and   I.
2. Ho!   John - ny   and   I.

The children stand in a circle, facing the center, with their joined hands raised to form arches. One child, the Bluebird, weaves in and out of the arches as the children sing verse one.

While the second verse is being sung, the Bluebird stops behind one of the players in the circle, tapping her on the shoulders with both hands. The child who has been tapped now joins the Bluebird and moves in front of her.

The first verse is sung again with the two players going in and out of the arches. The line grows by one each time the second verse is resung and the Bluebird taps another player. The tapping is continuous and each newcomer goes to the top of the line. When all are in line, the last person added taps the original Bluebird (who in turn is tapping the one in front of her, etc.) making the circle complete, one behind the other, all tapping with a rhythmic up-and-down motion as they sing.—*As played at Lost Creek School, Breathitt County, Kentucky. From "Circle Left."*

HOW MANY MILES TO BURNHAM BRIGHT?

8-20 players, 6-12 years   *Indoors or out of doors*

The children stand, hands joined, in a semicircle. Two children at one end of the line (A) speak alternate lines with the two at the other end of the line (B).

A: How many miles to Burnham Bright?
B: Three score and ten.
A: Can we get there by candlelight?
B. Yes, and back again.
A: Open the gates and let us go.
B: Not without your bow and bow (pronounced boo and bo).
A: Here's your bow (boo) and here's your bow (bo). Open the gates and let us go.

On "Here's your bow" (boo), the speakers (A) bend forward. On "And here's your bow" (bo), they bend backward.

After the words of the last line, they run very fast under the arch made by the two children on the opposite end (B), taking the entire line of children after them. The children hold hands all the time.

The game is repeated, changing sides or having new "speakers" as desired.—*As played at Tom's Branch School, Perry County, Kentucky. From "Circle Left."*

BOOGER MAN

6-30 players, 6-12 years   *Indoors or out of doors*

The Booger Man, behind a base line at one end of the playing space, faces the children standing behind a parallel base line at the other end about thirty feet away. They talk back and forth, using the following dialogue:

BOOGER MAN: What are you doing down there?
CHILDREN: Picking grapes.
BOOGER MAN: How big are they?
CHILDREN: Big as your head.
BOOGER MAN: How sweet are they?
CHILDREN: Sweet as honey.
BOOGER MAN: How sour are they?
CHILDREN: Sour as kraut.
BOOGER MAN: What would you do if you saw the Booger Man coming?
CHILDREN: Run like a turkey!

When the Booger Man asks the last question, the children run to his base line and he tags all he can before they can get to safety behind it. The action is repeated, with those tagged helping the Booger Man, until all are caught.—*As played at Stacy and Williams' Branch, Perry County, Kentucky. From "Circle Left."*

Spanish American Games

COBRA

10-30 children, 6-10 years   *Indoors or out of doors*

The players stand in a circle holding hands. One player is selected to be the Cobra and he stands in the center. He says, "Through which door shall I escape?" The players in the circle answer, "Not through here," and tighten their grip. The Cobra tries to press through the "doors" made by the clasped hands until he finally succeeds in getting out. The player whose hands slip to let him out is the next Cobra.—*From Manual School, Albuquerque, New Mexico.*

THE LITTLE BLIND CHICKEN

Indoors or out of doors   *Similar to Blindman's Buff*
6-20 players, 6-10 years

One child is chosen to be the Little Blind Chicken and he is blindfolded and placed in the center of a circle formed by the other children, who join hands and circle around him. The Little Blind Chicken tries to catch a child in the circle. When he catches one, he tries to guess his name. If he succeeds in doing this correctly, the child caught becomes the Little Blind Chicken. If he fails, he must try again.—*From Manual School, Albuquerque, New Mexico.*

THE KEY OF ROME AND TAKE IT
(Ésta es la Llave de Roma y Toma)

10-30 players, 8-12 years   *Indoors or out of doors*

The players form a circle and one of them has a key which he passes to the right. As he passes the key, he says to the one

accepting it, "This is the key of Rome and take it." Each person
in turn repeats the same phrase as he or she passes the key. The
one who fails to say the phrase correctly must pay a forfeit.
When the key has gone completely around the circle, it is
started again with the following phrases added in turn and repeated in the same manner as at first:

And in Rome there is a plaza,
In the plaza there is a street,
In the street there is a house,
In the house there is a bedroom,
In the bedroom there is a bird cage,
In the bird cage there is a parakeet that says:

(The phrases now added are the reverse of what has been
said before.)

The bird cage is not in the bedroom,
The bedroom is not in the house,
The house is not in the street,
The street is not in the plaza,
The plaza is not in Rome,
The key is not from Rome.

When all the phrases have been added, the game ends and
the forfeits are paid.—*Mr. José I. Candelaria, Albuquerque,
New Mexico.*

THE STICK

6-20 players, 8-12 years   *Indoors or out of doors*

A little stick that can be easily handled is selected and given
to one player. All players sit in a circle. The player with the
stick passes it to the one next him, saying, "Gentleman, here
is the stick; pass it to the gentleman." The second player passes
the stick along to the third, repeating the same words. After
the stick reaches the player who started it, he passes it again,
but this time he says, "Gentleman, here is one stick; two sticks;

pass them to the gentleman." Again these words are repeated around the circle. The third time round the words are "Gentleman, here is one stick; two sticks; three sticks; pass them to the gentleman." Round and round the circle goes the stick with new words added each time it goes around.

The first player to make a mistake has to be nicknamed. The players continue passing the stick until all are nicknamed. The last player to make a mistake is the winner.—*From Allison-James School, Santa Fé, New Mexico.*

Indian Games in the United States

The Indians of old were enthusiastic players of games. They often spent long hours, and at feast time even days, playing a single one. Some games were for men alone; some for women alone; and a few were for both. Certain ones were played at certain seasons or at set times of the day. The Indians had two types of games—games of skill and games of chance.

The children had games of their own. They also imitated the play of their elders. Since the Indian children are now being educated so widely in schools, they are forgetting many of their tribal games and learning those taught them by their teachers. But a number of the old tribal games are still being played today by men and women and children.

There was a certain similarity in many of the Indian games. "Stick Counting," "Hand Game," "Plum Pits," "Kick Ball," "Moccasin Game," "Buffalo Wheel," "Ring," and "Sticks" are games that were played with a few variations in most of the tribes by adults and by children in imitation. Though they are listed in this book under tribal divisions, they may be regarded as typical Indian games. The native names of the games have not been included because they are so difficult to pronounce. The name of the tribe is listed beside the title of the game.

In this section there will be found some adaptations of games that are common everywhere, such as "The Coyote and the Father." They are included because their adaptations are interesting and descriptive of the life of the people who have taken them over.

BUFFALO WHEEL: Arapaho

2-20 players, usually boys   *Out of doors*

The players use a wheel or hoop with rawhide strings tied over it in one direction and across it in another direction, until the space inside the wheel has been mostly covered. Many small square holes will remain open. From the center, each row of holes is given the name of some kind of animal. One boy stands at a distance and rolls the hoop toward another boy who is waiting for it to pass. This boy has a stick some three or four feet long. He throws the stick and tries to hit the center hole as the hoop passes. In the old days arrows were used. He is said to have hit the animal whose name has been given to the hole his stick touches. The hoop is rolled again and again until each player has had several turns. The boy who comes nearest the center the greatest number of times wins the game. Instead of the rawhide strings, strips of cotton cloth may be used, the strips being passed fully around the rim of the wheel and knotted at each turn.—*Miss Marguerite Cosgriff and classes at Haskell Institute, Lawrence, Kansas.*

HANDS AND BONES: Blackfoot

Indoors or out of doors   *Similar to Button, Button*
2-12 players, 8 years and up

The players are divided into two sides and seated in two lines opposite one another. The leader of one side takes two small oblong bones in his hands. One of the bones is plain and the other has a black ring around it. The leader changes the bones from one hand to the other, moving his hands and swaying his body, trying to make it impossible for his opponents to guess in which hand he holds the marked bone. If the opposing side guess right, they win a point. Ten points is the game. Two small sticks, one with a black mark on it, or a white and a black button, could be used instead of bones.—*From "Games of the North American Indians."*

JUMPING FROM SIDE TO SIDE: Cheyenne

6-20 players, 6-12 years   *Out of doors*

The children form in line with the tallest at the front and the others following in order of size, each one holding to the one in front of him. They dance along from side to side, jumping into the air with both feet, a little forward at each jump, and calling out in time, *"Hagh! Hagh! Hagh!"* If one of them laughs aloud, all the other children surround and pummel him. —*From "The Cheyenne Indians: Their History and Ways of Life."*

RUNNING THROUGH THE LINE: Cheyenne

Indoors or out of doors   *Similar to Bull in the Ring*
8-20 players, 8-12 years

The children stand in a circle, holding hands by locking the bent fingers of each hand in the bent fingers of the children on either side. It stands in the center of the ring. He keeps trying to break out of the circle by separating the handhold of two of the children. If he succeeds and escapes from the ring, all the others pursue him. Those who can overtake him clap him on the back with the open hand.—*From "The Cheyenne Indians: Their History and Ways of Life."*

PLAYING BEAR: Cheyenne

8-20 players, 6-12 years   *Out of doors*

A boy is chosen to be the Bear. He goes and hides in the brush or under a bush. The other boys and girls go to the place as if to gather fruit. While they are at work the Bear charges them. They cry out as he appears, "Look out for the Bear!" and all run away with the Bear chasing them. The Bear catches a child and pretends to be eating it. The boys gather about him and pretend to be shooting at him by throwing leaves at him and making noises like the explosion of a gun. At last the Bear appears to be killed and falls over. The players pretend to skin him and cut him up.—*From "The Cheyenne Indians: Their History and Ways of Life."*

STICK COUNTING: Chippewa

2-6 players, boys and men   *Indoors or out of doors*

The game may be played by two players, or by two sides with an even number of players. The players sit down opposite each other. Small sticks (toothpicks will suffice) are used as counters and each player has the same number. The player or the leader of the side having first turn holds up in front of him a bunch of eleven slender sticks. They are usually saplings about eleven inches long, which have been gaily painted. (A number of long pencils could be used instead.) Swiftly the player divides the bunch of sticks so that he holds five in one hand and six in the other. His opponent must quickly guess which hand holds the odd number of sticks, indicating his choice by touching the hand that he selects. If he guesses right, each one on his side wins a counter from the opposite team and he has the chance to guess again. If he guesses wrong, the long, slender sticks pass to him and each one on his side gives a counter to the one opposite him. If the game is played by sides, the other members of a team play in turn after the leader. The player or side that has the greatest number of counters at the end of a given time wins the game.—*From "Games of the North American Indians."*

STEALING STICKS: Choctaw

2-30 players, 6-12 years   *Indoors or out of doors*

Two sides of even number are chosen for this game. A straight line is drawn across the middle of the playing field. On each side of the line, at equal distances from it and exactly opposite each other, two circles are drawn, a large one at the upper end and a small one at the lower end of the line. Each small circle holds an equal number of sticks, which have been gathered by the players. The big circles are the mush pots to which the players who are caught must go.

At a given signal the game begins. Players run across the dividing line, try to steal sticks from the pile of the other team and return without being touched by the opponents. If they succeed, the sticks they bring are added to the home pile.

If they are touched by players of the opposite side before getting back across the center line, they must go to the mush pot and stay there until the game ends. The side that gets the most sticks in its pile wins the game.—*G. Harland Davis, Dwight Training School, Vian, Oklahoma.*

SNATCHING PLACES: Dakota

6-20 players   *Indoors or out of doors*

The players form a ring, each one standing upon his blanket, which marks his *owanka,* or place. (The places may be marked by a piece of cloth or paper.) The places should be about two feet apart. One player without a blanket stands in the center of the ring. The others constantly change places with one another, while the one in the center tries to step into a space left vacant for a moment. When he succeeds, the player displaced must stay in the center until he in turn is able to find a vacant place.—*From "Games of the Teton Dakota Children."*

THE SEEKER: Dakota

Out of doors   *Similar to Hide and Seek*
                    6-20 players, 8-12 years

One child is chosen to be It and the others hide. They whistle when they are ready. The Seeker, or *Wawole,* goes looking for them. Each child who is found becomes the servant of the *Wawole* and has to walk behind him while he seeks for the others. The various servants walk in single file behind their Master, in order of their capture, until all have been found. If there are over fifteen playing, there may be two or three Seekers.—*From "Games of the Teton Dakota Children."*

GRIZZLY BEAR GAME: Dakota

6-20 players, 8-12 years   *Out of doors*

One child is chosen to be the Grizzly Bear. He goes apart from the others, pretends to dig a hole for his den, and lies down in it. The other players crowd around him, one of them being selected as the leader on account of his bravery. The leader advances toward the Bear, with his followers behind him. The leader may dramatize his stealthy advance, now retiring a little, now going forward, while his followers do the same. Finally the leader gets close enough to the Bear to seize a lock of his hair. He says "Oh, Grandfather Grizzly Bear, here is a hair of your head!"

The Bear springs up and chases the players, who flee in all directions. When the Bear catches a player, he tickles him until he laughs heartily. The Bear never chases the children until the leader says the words, "Grizzly Bear." When the captive stops laughing, the Bear ceases tickling him. The Bear goes back to his den and lies down again. The players again crowd around him and the play is repeated.—*From "Games of the Teton Dakota Children."*

HAND GAME: Kickapoo

6-30 players, 10 years and up   *Indoors or out of doors*

This game is played with variations by many Indian tribes. Usually men and women do the playing, but children may play in imitation.

The women form one team and the men the other. Usually the women sit and the men stand. Each side has seven sticks that are used as counters.

A man from one side and a woman from the other stand in the middle of the players. The woman is given an object to be hidden. She puts her hands behind her and hides the object in one of her hands. Then she brings her hands forward and goes through various kinds of motions, sweeping her hands to and fro, keeping time to the chanting of the other players and the beating of a drum.

After waving her hands about for some time, the woman holds her hands out and the man is given a chance to guess in which hand the object is hidden. If he guesses correctly, a counting stick is given over to his side. If he fails in his guess, a counting stick from his side goes over to the woman's side.

Another man and woman then take the center and the hiding and guessing proceed. After a certain length of time, the players count their sticks. The side with the greatest number wins.—*Miss Marguerite Cosgriff and classes at Haskell Institute, Lawrence, Kansas.*

BATTLEDORE AND SHUTTLECOCK: Makah

1-12 players, boys, 8-14 years   *Indoors or out of doors*

The battledore is made of a round cedar board some eight inches in diameter and less than half an inch thick. The shuttlecock is made of a branch of salmon berry, in one end of which four duck feathers are thrust.

The boys take turns playing, each one having a chance to toss the shuttlecock and to keep it in the air as long as possible by striking it upward with the battledore.—*From "Games of the Makah Indians."*

BOUNCING STICKS: Navajo

2-30 players, boys and girls, 8 years and up   *Out of doors*

A number of small stones, about the size of a walnut, are placed on the ground to form a circle around a large rock in the center. The number of stones in the circle will depend upon the number of players. With three players, one hundred stones would be used. With a large number of players there might be one thousand stones. A starting place on the circle is agreed upon by the players. The object is to move around the circle in turns, marking moves by means of the stones in the circle. The first one to get around the circle and back to the starting place is the winner.

Three short, flat pieces of sticks about an inch and a half by five inches are used as counters. They are colored black on one side and white on the other. The first player throws the three sticks against the large rock in the center of the circle.

If the three white sides fall upward, the player counts five and has another turn. He then counts off five stones from the starting point and marks his place with a small stick. He takes another turn at throwing the sticks and moves again. After this the next player throws the sticks against the rock, perhaps counts three, makes his count, and marks his place with another small stick. The marking sticks of each player should be different from those of any other player, so they can be readily distinguished one from the other. The counts are decided by the color of the three sticks that are thrown against the rock. Three white sides upward is counted five and the player gets a second turn. Three black sides upward is counted three; that is, the player moves his marking stick three places. One black and two white sides is counted two. One white and two black sides upward is counted one.—*Miss Elma Smith, Ganado Mission, Arizona.*

THE COYOTE AND THE FATHER: Navajo

Out of doors   *Similar to Fox and Geese*
4-20 players, boys and girls, 6-12 years

One player is chosen to be the Coyote and another to be the Father. The rest of the players are Children. Usually the two tallest and oldest children are chosen to be the Coyote and the Father.

The children line up behind the Father. Usually the next oldest and tallest stand right behind the Father and the youngest or smallest at the end of the line. The players hold one another by the shoulders.

The Coyote stands facing the Father. The following dialogue takes place:

COYOTE: I've come to get John (if John is the first in line).

FATHER: No, I can't spare John because he herds the sheep and I can't get along without him.

COYOTE: May I have Mary then (if Mary is the second in line)?

FATHER: No, you can't have Mary, because she weaves rugs.

The Coyote asks the Father for each child in the line, calling each by name. The Father refuses each request, saying that Jim has to carry water, Jane has to wash dishes, Jack has to bring in the fuel, Anne has to grind corn, Bill has to get the horse, Sarah has to mind the baby. The Father having refused to give up any of his children, the Coyote starts to catch the one at the end of the line. The Father, with his line of children following his every move, tries to protect the child under attack.

When the child at the end of the line is touched by the Coyote, he drops out of the game. When the Coyote has caught all of the Children, he chases the Father. As soon as he has caught him, the Coyote begins to run from the Father, who now chases him. The game ends when the Father succeeds in catching the Coyote.—*Miss Elma Smith, Ganado Mission, Arizona.*

RING AND PIN: Navajo

1 or more players, 8-16 years   *Indoors or out of doors*

This is a game for individuals. It will be enjoyed by a group playing in turns. A ring about five inches in diameter is needed. It may be made of twisted twigs and wrapped with a bright-colored yarn, usually blue. The ring is tied with the yarn to a stick about twenty-one inches long. The object of the game is to toss the ring into the air and catch it on the stick. Navajo children become very expert at this game.—*From "Games of the North American Indians."*

RING: Navajo

2-20 players, 8-12 years   *Out of doors*

The game is played with a twig ring, four and a half inches in diameter, wrapped with the fibers of yucca leaves, half of the ring being painted and half being left green. Two stakes about a foot high are stuck into the ground as pegs, being placed about as far apart as a boy can pitch the ring.

The players line up and start pitching in turn. The thrower stands by one peg and tries to toss the ring close to or over the other peg. If the ring falls so that its white side touches the peg, it counts one. If the green side touches, it counts two. The players need to settle upon the number of points (say ten) that are necessary to win the game. If a player tosses the ring over the peg, he counts ten (or number decided upon) and has won the game.—*From "Games of the North American Indians."*

HIDING THE THIMBLE: Osage

6-15 players, 6-12 years   *Indoors*

A small beaded thimble made out of buckskin is used as the article to be hidden. The purpose of the game is to see who can make the highest score.

The players sit in a circle. The person who is It stands in the center and the scorekeeper stands at the side. He writes the names of the players on paper or on the blackboard and keeps the score. It takes the thimble and gives it to one of the players. The player takes the thimble and hides it in one of his hands. It guesses in which hand he has it. If It guesses wrong, the player scores a point and hides the thimble again. The player gets as many scores as It guesses wrong. When It guesses right, he moves on to the next player and the next until he goes around the circle two or three times. When the scorekeeper adds up the scores, the person who has the most points is the winner.—*Miss Jennie Gott, Elbowoods, North Dakota.*

ROCK JACKS: Paiute

2-6 players, boys and girls, 8-12 years   *Out of doors*

"When I was a little girl living in Virginia City, Nevada, which must have been over thirty-seven years ago, we Paiute Indian girls and boys played several games and from among them I am going to tell you about one which you might like to play.

"The game can have two or more players, but we usually had four boys and girls in our games. We would find and put in a pile a number of rocks, each about the size of your hand. Sometimes a few of the rocks would be a little oversized, but they would never be so large that two rocks could not be held in the hand at once. The pile could have just as many rocks in it as we cared to have. Of course, the larger the pile of rocks, the longer we would have to play until the game was completed.

"We would sometimes take pride in getting the prettiest 'tough' rock, which was used for tossing into the air. These would be of beautifully colored Nevada rocks and would often take a long time to find.

"When the game was ready to begin, we would all sit on the ground around the pile of rocks we had gathered. The first person would start by throwing his 'tough' rock into the air. While it was in the air, he would reach for one of the rocks in the pile and catch his 'tough' rock as it came down. He would place in front of him the rock he had taken and then throw again. You see, you have to be very quick, and sometimes when you reach for a rock in the pile, you miss the small one and must take the rock your hand touches. The player continues until he misses, and then the second player begins. He plays until he misses, and the game goes on until all the rocks have been taken from the center pile.

"The game might end here, the one with the most rocks being the winner. We used to go further, playing against one another's pile of rocks, each taking his or her turn until one player in the game had secured all the rocks. Each in turn we would place a rock from our piles in the center of the ring to be picked up by the player who was throwing. It was great fun to see how each player would try hard to be the one to secure all the rocks. You see, when we played against one another, we could choose the rock to put in the center for our opponent to pick up while his 'tough' rock was in the air. Sometimes I would put my largest rock there, making it difficult for him to hold both it and his 'tough' rock at the same time."—*Dictated to the Reverend Floyd O. Burnett by a Paiute Indian mother, Mrs. Amy Higgins, of Schurz, Nevada.*

HANDS: Pawnee

Indoors or out of doors   *Similar to Button, Button*
12-30 players, 10-14 years

The players are divided into sides and each chooses a leader. Each player gets himself a number of small, slender sticks, usually ten, as counters. (Toothpicks will make good counters.) The players sit down opposite each other, three or four feet apart. The leader of the side that has first turn takes a pebble or small object and passes it to the person next to him, who hands it on down the line. False passes are made to confuse the leader of the opposite side, who must guess which player holds the object by pointing at him. If he guesses correctly, he gets the object for his side to hide. If he guesses wrong, his opponents keep the object and he and his players must each give a counter to the one sitting opposite. The game goes on until one side has all the sticks.—*From "Games of the North American Indians."*

VAPUTTA: Pima

12-30 players, usually boys, 10-16 years   *Out of doors*

The players are divided into teams and a leader is chosen for each. The teams line up facing each other a few feet apart. A goal is marked off about fifty yards distant from the first player on each team. The leader of the team that has first turn walks along behind his players, carrying a pebble or some small object in his hand. He pretends to place it in the hand of several players as he passes along, and actually does place it in one hand. When he reaches the end of the line, the leader of the opposite side guesses which player has the pebble or object. If he guesses right, he takes the object to hide in the hands of his team. If he guesses wrong, the player at the far end of the line having the object runs and jumps over the upheld leg of the man at the head of the line. This moves his side one man and the length of the jump nearer to the goal. The same leader hides the pebble once more and the play continues. The side that first reaches the goal wins the game.—*From "Games of the North American Indians."*

KICK BALL: Plains Indians

2-20 players, women or girls   *Indoors or out of doors*

A ball is made out of strips of cloth wound around a small rock. There should be enough cloth to give bounce to the ball.

When the ball is the desired size, a large piece of cloth is sewed around it as a cover. A large rubber ball or basketball could be used in place of the cloth ball.

Two people may play the game and see who can kick the ball the highest number of times. Or a larger number may play, taking turns one after another. The first player kicks until she misses the ball, then passes the ball to the next person. The game proceeds until the last player has her chance. The person who keeps kicking the ball on her foot the longest is the winner.

The first player must ask the other player what type of kick she wants to play. The same type of kick is used throughout. There are several kinds of kicks. The plain kick is the most common. The ball is held in the hand, dropped to the foot, and then kicked upward. As it comes down, it is kicked upward again. Each time the ball touches the foot, the player counts one. As soon as the player misses the ball, her turn ends.

Touching the ground is another kind of kick. The ball is dropped from hand to foot as before and kicked upward. The player stoops and touches the ground while the ball is in the air, straightens up, and kicks the ball upward as it comes down. This also is kept up until the ball is missed.—*Miss Marguerite Cosgriff and classes at Haskell Institute, Lawrence, Kansas.*

MOCCASIN GAME: Plains Indians

4-6 players, usually men or boys   *Indoors or out of doors*

This game is very common among the Sioux, Chippewa, and Omaha Indians, and variations of it are found in almost every other tribe. The men play this game and the women watch as onlookers. Children may imitate the play. In former years four moccasins were used in the game. Nowadays four squares of cloth may take the place of the moccasins.

Four marbles or small stones are used for hiding under the moccasins or bits of cloth. Three should be of the same color and the fourth of a different color or with a different marking.

The players are divided into sides, two or three to a side. The players sit in pairs across from each other. Each side has about ten sticks to be used as counters. Two players sitting opposite each other start the play. One hides the marbles, one under each moccasin or bit of cloth. He tries to do it in such a manner that his opponent cannot see where he places the marked marble.

The opponent has a long stick, with which he may turn over any two moccasins or pieces of cloth. He tries to turn over the one under which the marked marble is hidden. If he succeeds, his side has the next turn with the marbles. If he fails, a counting stick from his side is turned over to the other side.

While the game is going on, the persons who are waiting for their turn to play keep up a chant, which is accompanied by the beat of drums. At the end of the game the sticks are counted. The side with the greatest number wins.—*Miss Marguerite Cosgriff and classes at Haskell Institute, Lawrence, Kansas.*

DODGE BALL: Pueblo

10-30 players, boys and girls, 10-14 years   Indoors or out of doors

A soft ball or a beanbag is used in this game. Two leaders are chosen who select their teams. Each team should contain an equal number of players. The teams stand in parallel lines about twelve feet apart. The first player in Team I steps forward a few feet from the line. The first player in Team II throws the soft ball at him, trying to hit him. The player from Team I tries to dodge the ball. He may duck any way he wishes, stooping, twisting, right or left; but he may not move his feet. If he is hit by the ball, he must go over to the opposite team. If the player from Team II fails to hit him, that player must go over to Team I. The second player in Team I then steps forward and the second player in Team II tries to hit him. After each player in Team II has had a chance to hit a member of Team I, the ball is passed to the other side for throwing. Team I now tries to hit the members of Team II in turn. The team that wins the greatest number of players from the opposite side is the winner.—*Mrs. Mabel Analla, Laguna Pueblo Reservation, Seama Village, Cubero, New Mexico.*

THE COYOTE AND THE SHEEP: Pueblo

Indoors or out of doors   *Similar to Fox and Geese*
6-20 players, boys and girls, 6 years up

One player is chosen to be the Coyote and another to be the Mother Sheep. The Coyote selects a den and there he stays. The Mother Sheep approaches him with outstretched arms. The other players are her Sheep and follow behind her, each holding the one in front around the waist. The following dialogue takes place:

MOTHER SHEEP: How do you do, Mr. Coyote? What are you looking for?

COYOTE: How do you do? I am looking for my sheep.

MOTHER SHEEP: What do your sheep look like?

The Coyote peeps around the Mother Sheep and then describes any of the Sheep in the line, telling the color of the clothes.

MOTHER SHEEP: Try and get your sheep, Mr. Coyote.

The Coyote tries to get the Sheep, but the Mother tries to protect her flock with her outstretched arms. When the Coyote catches a Sheep he takes it to his den, where it must stay. The game proceeds until all the Sheep have been described and caught.—*Mrs. Mabel Analla, Laguna Pueblo Reservation, Seama Village, Cubero, New Mexico.*

HIDDEN BALL: Pueblo

Boys, 10 years up to adults   *Indoors or out of doors*

Two leaders are selected and they in turn choose sides. There should be an equal number of players.

The articles needed for the game are a stone, bean, or marble, an even number of cups (four or more) or containers, and a sheet or blanket to hold between the two groups while the object is being hidden.

The cups are turned upside down on the floor or ground. The players group themselves around their leaders. One group hides the ball or bean in one of the cups, behind the protection of the blanket. The other group chooses a member to guess where it is hidden. If the guess is right, the guesser's team scores a point. If wrong, the hider's side scores one. The guesser may be allowed to tap a little on the cups, so that the resulting sound may guide him in his guess. The stone changes from one side to the other with each correct guess.

This game is connected with religious ritual to some extent and is played only in the winter.—*Mrs. Mabel Analla, Laguna Pueblo Reservation, Seama Village, Cubero, New Mexico.*

KICKING THE STICK: Pueblo

Boys, 8 years up to adults   *Out of doors*

In the early days, the young men were required to run for many miles every morning to enable them to become fast runners and strong at bearing heat and cold. Kicking the stick is one of the games they used for training. Adults usually ran for several miles out of the village before they started homeward.

Two sticks about four inches long and one inch in diameter are used in the game. Two leaders are selected, who in turn choose sides. The players stand in parallel lines behind their leaders. A line is drawn in front of the leaders and on this line the sticks are laid, one in front of each team. At a given signal, the leaders run forward and kick the sticks as hard as they can, each one taking the stick in front of his team. The rest of the players follow, getting into the race by taking their turn at kicking the stick whenever they get a chance. The players must not pick up the sticks at any time. They must kick them out of any brush or hole that they may get into. Before the race a goal must be decided upon, at which place the players are to turn homeward. The players must all pass this goal before they turn about and go in the other direction. If they fail to pass it, they cannot kick the stick again. The first team to kick its stick back to the starting place is winner.

The women and other folks of the village who do not participate in this race usually stand at the starting place to cheer the winners.—*Mrs. Mabel Analla, Laguna Pueblo Reservation, Seama Village, Cubero, New Mexico.*

STICKS: Ute

2-20 players, 9 years and up   *Indoors or out of doors*

The game of Sticks is a game universally loved by the Indians and played in many different ways. The players sit on the ground facing each other. The onlookers watch with interest and chant songs. Each player holds in his hand a small stick, stone, seed, or some other small object. Each player tries to guess in which hand the player opposite is holding the object. If he guesses correctly, he counts a point. If he guesses wrong, his opponent gains a point. The counting is often done by means of small, slender sticks. The player collects a stick from his opponent for each point he makes. When the game ends, the player who has won the most points (or sticks) is declared the winner.—*Girls at Sherman Institute, Riverside, California.*

MY OLD INDIAN: Ute

12-40 players, boys and girls, 10-16 years   Indoors or out of doors

The girls and boys divide into separate groups, equal in numbers. The boys choose a Chief and the girls a Princess. The Chief numbers the boys secretly and the Princess numbers the girls secretly. The Chief and Princess decide ahead of time what forfeits shall be paid and how. Then they each call out a number, the Chief to the boys, the Princess to the girls. The boy and girl with those numbers must take a stand some twelve feet or more apart, face each other, and walk toward each other. Just as they are to pass each other, the girl says, "My Old Indian," and the boy says, "My Old Squaw." If either laughs, he has to pay the forfeit right then. Everyone watches while they do it. When the forfeit is paid, the Chief and Princess each call another number and the game proceeds as before until all have had a chance to play. The penalty is usually a stunt demanded by the Chief and the Princess. —*Girls at Sherman Institute, Riverside, California.*

PLUM PITS: Winnebago

2, 4, or more players, girls or women   Indoors or out of doors

This game is played only by women and girls. A wooden bowl and eight flat, round pieces of wood or bone about one inch in diameter are used. Probably at one time plum pits were used in the bowl. The Sioux women play a similar game with peach pits. The wood or bone pieces are darkened on one side by soot or paint and one piece has a special mark on each side. Each player has ten long slender sticks as counters. The players sit down opposite each other in pairs, only an even number being allowed. The others are spectators and watch. A player on one side has the first toss. Then the bowl is passed to the opposite player. The play passes from one side to the other in succession. The play consists of shaking the eight pieces in the bowl, tossing them some eight or ten inches into the air, and allowing them to fall back into the bowl. The count is made according to the number of dark and white sides that fall uppermost, as follows:

Ten points are counted when there are seven white sides and the dark side of the special piece showing; and also when there are seven dark sides and the white side of the special piece showing. Four points are counted when either eight dark or eight white sides show. Two points are counted when one dark and seven white, seven dark and one white, two dark and six white, or six dark, one white, and the white side of the special piece show. One point is counted when six dark and two white show. No points are counted when three dark and five white, four dark and four white, or five dark and three white show.

The player collects from her opponent counting sticks to the value of her throw. The side that gains all the counters wins the game.—*Benjamin Stucki, Winnebago Indian Mission, Wisconsin.*

BALL RACE: Zuñi

6-20 players, 8-12 years   *Out of doors*

The players are divided into two sides, facing a goal some thirty feet away. Each player has a stick of wood and a ball or even a stone the size of a fist, which he knocks toward the goal with the stick. The side that gets all its balls or stones across the goal line first wins. The sticks used should be about five inches long and one inch thick. Indian boys often decorate these sticks by painting or carving them.—*From "Games of the North American Indians."*

SHUTTLECOCK: Zuñi

1-20 players, boys, 8-12 years   *Indoors or out of doors*

This is a game that the Zuñis claim originated with them. It is played in only one other district in the country. For the shuttlecock the children make a little square of about one and a half inches, constructed of corn husks, neatly interlaced with two feathers projecting from the center of one side.

One player tosses the shuttlecock into the air, knocking it upward again and again with the palm of his hand. It makes a sound like the noise of a rabbit's tread on frozen snow. When the shuttlecock falls to the ground, the player picks it up and tosses it again. Usually each boy has ten tosses before the play passes to the next in line. Of course, each boy tries to keep the shuttlecock in the air as long as possible after each toss.—*From "Games of the North American Indians."*

Games from Europe

EUROPE is the source of most of the games played by the children of North and South America. This is reasonable enough since the white settlers of the Americas came almost wholly from Europe. In Latin America the games have largely a Spanish origin. In the United States and Canada many of the games are the same as those played in the British Isles, the common language making such a transfer practical. Such well known games as "Drop the Handkerchief," "London Bridge," "Fox and Geese," and "Kick the Can" came from the British Isles. Of course, the same games were played in other countries of Europe. Indeed, it is difficult to tell from which countries the games originally came. Some of them are ancient and widespread. "The Spanish Knight," for instance, is a very old game and variations of it are to be found in England, France, Iceland, Italy, Finland, and Scotland. "The Mulberry Bush" is likewise an old and popular game.

Some of the games of Europe were played at harvest time by the young people after they had finished their work in the fields. "Cut the Oats," in Norway, and "Barley Break," in England and in Germany, are examples of games with a seasonal origin.

Games from the non-English-speaking parts of Europe have been adapted over the years for play by the boys and girls of this country. "Chicken Market" from Italy, "Prince of Paris" from France, and "Gorelki" from Russia are commonly played here. In the selection of games that follow, an attempt has been made to include the less well known ones, so that children's play experience may be broadened.

Austria

RESTAURANT
(Caféhaus)

6-30 players, 8-12 years   *Indoors*

One of the group is chosen to tell a story about a restaurant, or the leader may tell the story. The players sit in a circle and each one is given the name of something that is to be found in a restaurant, such as milk, coffee, waiter, table, cake, and so forth. It stands or sits in the center of the circle and tells a story, mentioning the word "restaurant" frequently, and also the names of the things that are found in a restaurant. When "restaurant" is mentioned, everyone in the circle claps his hands. When a name is mentioned that has been given to one of the players, such as milk, that player must clap his hands. When a player fails to clap in the right place, he must give a forfeit, which is redeemed after the story.—*Miss Celia Gruener.*

NUMBERS
(Nummernspiel)

Indoors or out of doors   *Similar to Blindman's Buff*
6-30 players, 7-10 years

One child is chosen to be It. He is blindfolded and put in the center of a circle of children who are sitting on the ground. Each player in the circle takes a number, beginning with one and going up. It calls out two of the numbers. The players who have those numbers must change places immediately. They try to do it as silently as possible, so that their movements will not be detected by It, who tries to catch one of them. If they reach their new places safely, everyone in the circle claps hands and It must try again. If one of them is

caught, he must change places with It and the game goes on.
—*Miss Celia Gruener.*

Czechoslovakia

CONFESSIONS
(Zpoved)

Indoors   *Similar to Forfeits*
6-20 players, 6-8 years

One player is chosen to stand with his back to the others.
The leader or an older child asks him questions, which he is
to answer by "Yes" or "No," or by "Once" or "Never." The
leader says aloud only part of the question, acting out the other
part so that the players can see him. The questions and acting
should be humorous, such as, "Do you do this every day (acting out the washing of the face)?" or "How many times do
you do this (acting out the brushing of the teeth)?" The idea
is to make the questions, motions, and answers as ridiculous
as possible. All the players in turn must answer questions.—
*Miss Anita Blaukopf, Prague, Czechoslovakia, and New York
City.*

HIDE THE THIMBLE

5-15 players, 6-8 years   *Indoors*

A small object, such as a thimble, penny, or button, is chosen
to be hidden and all the players but the one who is It leave
the room. It hides the object and then calls the players back
into the room. If It sees any player nearing the object, he calls,
"Warm." If the players are going away from the object, he
calls, "Water." If they go farther away, he calls, "Water, water,
you will drown." As they get closer and closer to the object, he
calls, "Warm, warm, you will burn." The players must decide

for themselves which of them is close enough to the object to "burn." The player finding the object is the next It.—*Miss Anita Blaukopf, Prague, Czechoslovakia, and New York City.*

Denmark

THE TROLL HEAD

10-25 players, 6-10 years   *Indoors or out of doors*

The outline of a huge troll's head, with a large nose and ears and high forehead and long teeth, is drawn on the ground with a stick or on the floor with chalk. (A troll is a kind of ogre, and in some stories trolls eat children.) The players take their places along the outline. The leader gives a loud groan or shriek and all the children try to push each other off the line. If a child gets pushed inside the head, it means that the troll has eaten him, and therefore he is out of the game. The children must keep their arms folded over their chests while they are pushing. The pushing is done with the body alone. Several players may push a single one over the line. The player who is left alone on the line is the winner.

THE FISH GAME

6-30 players   *Indoors or out of doors*

The players are divided into couples. One couple is chosen to be It and they are called Whales. Each of the other couples secretly selects the name of a fish. These couples get chairs for themselves and place them in pairs about the room.

The Whales walk about the room calling the names of fish. Whenever the name of a fish chosen by a couple is called out, that pair must rise from their chairs and march behind the Whales. The Whales march and call out as many fish names as they wish or know, then they say, "The ocean is calm!" All the players rise from their seats and march behind the Whales, who lead the line of players weaving in and out among the chairs. Suddenly the Whales call, "The ocean is stormy!" All the players run in pairs to get chairs. The couple left without seats become Whales for the next game.

England

BARLEY BREAK

6, 12, or 18 players, 9-14 years   *Indoors or out of doors*

This game used to be played in the barley fields at harvest time, one couple taking the part of two farmers guarding the fields and the others acting as trespassers who try to tramp down the barley.

A playing field is marked out in three equal divisions, each some twenty to forty feet square. The central square is the "barley field" and in it two players stand with linked arms, facing in opposite directions. A couple stand in each of the other squares and they are the "barley breakers." If more than six want to play, two or three couples may be placed in each square.

The couples from the side squares go forward into the barley field, either singly or in pairs, calling out, "Barley break!" They run and skip around the field pretending to trample down the barley while the two who are guarding the field try to catch them. If one player is caught, he must stand still in the barley field until his partner also is caught. The guards of the field may not leave their square nor may the opposing couples run for safety to any square but their own. It is more fun to catch one of each of the couples playing, before going on to capture their partners. When two partners have been caught, they become the guardians of the field. Those who have had to stand in the field because they have been caught return to their own squares. The former guardians take the square belonging to the couple caught and the game proceeds. In running, the guardians should always move as a pair.

KICKERY

Indoors or out of doors   *Similar to Hide and Seek*
6-20 players, 10-16 years

One player is chosen to be It and he should choose a rather large place in which to hide. In this game, It's object is to hide from the others, not to seek them. While someone counts to a hundred, It hurries off and hides. At the end of the count, the seekers call, "Coming," and the hunt begins. The seekers should spread out for the hunting. As soon as a hunter finds the hidden one, he stays quietly in the same place. Usually one player after another comes until all have discovered the hidden one. The one who last discovers the hidden player becomes the next It. If he cannot find them, he may call, "Give up," and then he must hide while the others hunt for him.—*Miss Edith Creighton, Halifax, Canada.*

THE MUFFIN MAN

10-30 players, 6-9 years   *Indoors or out of doors*

The players form a circle with one child standing in the center. The children dance around the circle as they sing the first half of the verse. They stand still and begin to sing the second half. The child in the center chooses a partner and joins hands with him. The two of them dance around inside the circle while the rest of the verse is sung. At the end of the verse the child who did the choosing goes back to the ring. The partner now stands in the center, the verse is sung again, and the game proceeds.

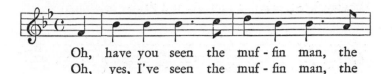

Oh,   have you   seen   the   muf - fin   man,   the
Oh,   yes, I've   seen   the   muf - fin   man,   the

muf-fin man, the muf - fin man? Oh, have you seen the
muf-fin man, the muf - fin man. Oh, yes, I've seen the

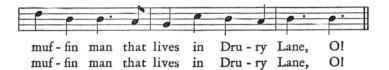

muf - fin man that lives in Dru - ry Lane, O!
muf - fin man that lives in Dru - ry Lane, O!

THE MULBERRY BUSH

8-30 players, usually girls, 6-12 years   *Indoors or out of doors*

The children form a ring, clasping hands and circling around as they sing the first verse, which is repeated between each of the other verses as a refrain. In the second and succeeding ones, the children stand still and pantomime the action described in the words.

> This is the way we wash our clothes,
> We wash our clothes, we wash our clothes.
> This is the way we wash our clothes,
> So early Monday morning.

The words "we wash our clothes" become "we iron our clothes," "we scrub our floor," "we mend our clothes," "we sweep the house" in the following verses; and Monday becomes Tuesday, Wednesday, Thursday, and Friday morning.

Here   we   go round the   mul - ber - ry bush, the

mul - ber - ry   bush,   the   mul - ber - ry   bush.

Here   we   go round   the   mul - ber - ry bush,   so

ear - ly   i - n   the   morn - ing.

France

MY GREAT AUNT LIVES IN TOURS

2-15 players, 5-8 years   *Indoors or out of doors*

The children sit informally and repeat the words of the rhyme in chorus, making appropriate sounds after each animal named. Any number of animals and birds may be added to the jingle.

My great aunt lives in Tours,
In a house with a cherry tree,
With a little mouse (squeak, squeak)
And a great big dog (bow, wow)
And a tabby cat (miaow, miaow)
And a speckled hen (cluck, cluck)
And a small pink pig (oink, oink)
And a spotted cow (moo, moo).

PRINCE OF PARIS

10-30 players, boys or girls, 8-12 years   Indoors or out of doors

One player is chosen to be It and the others are given numbers beginning with one and going up. It stands in front of the players, who are seated in a row with their arms folded across their chests. It says, "The Prince of Paris has lost his hat. Did you find it, Number Five, sir?" (or any other number that he selects). At these words, Number Five leaps to his feet and says, "What, sir! I, sir?"

It: Yes, sir, you, sir.
Five: Not I, sir!
It: Who then, sir?
Five: Number Six, sir (or any other number that he selects).
Six (as soon as he is called, he leaps up and says): What, sir! I, sir?

It tries to say, "The Prince of Paris has lost his hat," before Number Six (or an other number called) can jump to his feet and say, "What, sir! I, sir?" If It succeeds, he changes places with the player who has been slow to leap up and reply. If the player is alert and It does not succeed in repeating his words first, the dialogue proceeds as given and Number Six calls the number of another player to carry on the game. If a player fails to say "sir" at the proper time, he has to change places with It.

HIDE, HIDE
(Cache-Cache)

Indoors or out of doors　　　　　　　*Similar to Hide and Seek*
5-30 players, boys and girls, 8-14 years

One player is selected to be It. A goal is chosen. It stands at the goal, turns his back or hides his face and counts to one hundred. While he is counting, the rest of the players hide at some distance from the goal. It goes to look for them.

In this game the players do not remain in their first hiding place. They try to get nearer and nearer the goal by moving from one hiding place to another without letting It see them. If It sees a player moving or hiding, he calls his name aloud. If the player is too far from the goal to reach it before It does, he is counted out. If the player is near enough to the goal to have a chance at reaching it before It does, he calls loudly, *"Cache-cache!"* and races for the goal. It tries to tag or trip him on the way. If It catches him, that player becomes the next It and the game begins all over again. If It fails to catch him, he tries to get the next player who calls, *"Cache-cache!"* If he fails to catch anyone, he is It again for another turn.

Germany

LITTLE HANS
(Haenschen Klein)

8-24 players, 6-10 years　　　　　　*Indoors or out of doors*

The children form a circle. One player is chosen to be Little Hans and he is given a stick and hat. Other players are chosen to be the Mother, the Sister, and three Neighbors. They stand in the circle until the singing of verse three.

Hans walks gaily around inside the circle during the singing of the first half of verse one. Then he leaves the circle and his Mother waves to him during the singing of the next half.

As verse two is sung, Little Hans approaches the circle. He enters the circle as the first line of verse three is sung.

The three Neighbors and his Sister walk past him shaking their heads and then the Mother comes and greets him joyously.

Lit - tle Hans goes a - lone out in - to the wide, wide world. Hat on head, stick in hand, he is ver - y gay. Yet his moth - er's heart is sad; she will lose her lit - tle lad. "Good-by, Son," she calls out, "come back out some day."

Seven years, little Hans wanders round the wide, wide world.
Now he's grown, straight and tall, strong of heart and will.
Then his thoughts turn toward his home.
He has no more wish to roam.
"When I'm back," wonders Hans, "will they know me still?"

One, two, three, pass him by. This tall Hans is strange to them.
Sister says, "A fine face! Who can this man be?"
Then his mother comes along,
Sees him standing, straight and strong.
"Hans, my son," she cries out, "you've come back to me!"

The game may be played over and over with different players taking the parts of Hans, his Mother, and the others. —*Mrs. Frederick Flothmeier, Philadelphia, Pennsylvania.*

ADAM HAD SEVEN SONS

6-20 players, boys and girls, 6-11 years   *Indoors or out of doors*

The children form a circle with the player who has been chosen to be It in the center. All then chant or sing this song:

> Adam had seven sons,
> Seven sons had Adam.
> The seven sons were gay and glad,
> They did just as Adam bade.
> "All do as I do," said Adam.

As they sing the words of the last line, the children watch It and do just as he does. It may pretend to be a rooster crowing and flapping his wings, a hen scratching gravel and clucking, a frog or toad hopping, a donkey flapping his long ears, a cow chewing her cud, and so forth. He may change quickly from one to the other. The players must change quickly, too. Any player who fails to do as It does must change places with him.

RINGEL, RINGEL
(Ringel, Ringel)

Indoors or out of doors   *Similar to Ring around a Rosy*
4-20 players, 4-8 years

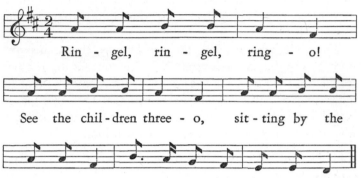

Rin - gel, rin - gel, ring - o!

See the chil - dren three - o, sit - ting by the

li - lac bush. Call to- geth - er, hush, hush, hush!

The children form in a ring and go dancing around in a circle. On the words "Hush, hush, hush," they all squat down. The game is played over and over.—*Mrs. Frederick Flothmeier, Philadelphia, Pennsylvania.*

Greece

PEBBLE

Indoors or out of doors   *Similar to Hide the Button*
6-20 players, 6-12 years

One player is chosen to be It and he is given a small pebble. The others stand in line with their hands held out, palms together and thumbs up. It selects a goal some twenty or thirty feet from the line.

It walks along the line and pretends to drop a pebble into each player's hands. Somewhere along the line he actually does drop the pebble into a child's hands. That child must do the running. The other children chase him while It stands still. The child with the pebble tries to get to the goal and back to It without being caught. If he succeeds, he becomes It for the next game. If he is caught, the one who captured him becomes the next It.

The child who receives the pebble may choose his own time to run, but he must start before It touches the last pair of hands in the line. He tries to look unconcerned so that the others will not guess that he has the pebble. The other players watch carefully and try to guess which one has the pebble so that they may be ready to chase and catch him.

Holland

CAPTURED
(Prooi)

Indoors   *Similar to Hide and Seek*
8-20 players, boys and girls, 10-16 years

The leader cuts out as many little pieces of paper as there are children. On one piece is written the word *Prooi* (prō-ĭ). All the others are left blank. The papers are placed on a plate, with the marked paper hidden among them blank side up. The plate is passed and each player draws a piece of paper. The child who draws the marked paper becomes the *Prooi*. The lights are put out and the children move around in the dark.

The child who is the *Prooi* hides himself in not too difficult a place and there he remains for the rest of the game. The

other players move around. When they touch another, they ask, *"Prooi?"* All players who are not the real *Prooi* must answer, *"Prooi."* The players keep moving, touching, and questioning one another. When the real *Prooi* is touched and questioned, he gives no answer. He takes the player who has touched him by the hand and both stand together. When other players question them, neither answers, but their hands are taken and all stand together. Each child who touches any of them joins the silent group. Finally the lights are turned on and a count is made to see if all players have been caught. To play the game again, the papers must be passed anew.
—*Miss Catherina Fruin, Holland and the United States.*

IN HOLLAND STANDS A HOUSE
(In Holland Staat een Huis)

Indoors or out of doors   Similar to Farmer in the Dell
10-30 players, boys and girls, 6-12 years

The game begins in much the same way as our "Farmer in the Dell," and the same tune may be used with the translation of the song given here. The first verse goes:

> In Holland stands a house *(In Holland staat een huis),*
> In Holland stands a house,
> Jig, jiggety, ting-a-ling,
> In Holland stands a house.

The following verses announce in turn that "In the house there's a man" *(In dat huis daar woon un man,* etc.); "The man takes a wife, etc."; "The wife takes a child, etc."; "The child takes a maid, etc."; "The maid takes a cat, etc."; "The cat takes a mouse."

In playing the game, the players take hands and move in a circle singing. At the words "In the house there is a man," a boy who has been previously chosen for the part leaves the circle and stands· in the center. He chooses a girl for a wife, who in turn chooses a child, and so on. The ones in the center form a small circle inside the large one, moving around and singing.

After the mouse is chosen, the game becomes different from "The Farmer in the Dell." The children sing, "We chase the man from the house, etc.," and the man leaves the little circle for the large one. The wife and the maid are also chased from the house, as the children sing verses to that effect. Then the children sing, "The cat eats the mouse," as the cat and mouse join the big circle. Now only the child is left in the center and the group sings, "We set fire to the house." As they sing, the children hold their hands out with the first fingers pointing outward. They move the right first finger down the left, as if making shavings. They move toward the child at the center of the circle. At the end of that verse the game ends.—*Miss Catherina Fruin, Holland and the United States.*

ALL THE BIRDS FLY
(Alle Vogels Vliegen)

Indoors   *Similar to Simon Says*
6-20 players, boys and girls, 6-10 years

The players are usually seated around a table. The leader says, "All the birds fly," and the children raise both arms as if to fly. It speaks quickly and mentions many things that fly and some that do not. He may say that all pigeons fly, airplanes fly, elephants fly, and so on. The children are supposed to raise their arms when things that really fly are mentioned and to keep their arms down when things that do not fly are named.

A child who has made a mistake must pay a forfeit, or *pand* as it is called. The game usually goes on until every child has given at least one forfeit. The forfeits are piled on the table and covered with a handkerchief. The leader touches one through the handkerchief and asks what the child who owns it must do to get it back. The group may suggest such things as singing a song or going out of the room or kissing the wall. When the action is done, the child gets his forfeit back. All the players win their forfeits back in this way. The game may then end or be played over again.—*Miss Catherina Fruin, Holland and the United States.*

Italy

CHICKEN MARKET

8-20 players, 6-10 years   *Indoors or out of doors*

One child is chosen to be the Market Woman and another the Buyer. The rest of the children pretend that they are Chickens. The Chickens stand in a row behind the Market Woman. They stoop down and clasp their hands under their knees. This position they hold during the game.

The Buyer comes up to the Market Woman and the following conversation takes place:

BUYER: Have you any chickens?

MARKET WOMAN: Yes, I have some good chickens. Would you like to try them?

BUYER: If you please.

Then the Buyer goes behind one Chicken after another in the line, prodding them. "This is too fat," he says of one. "This is too skinny," "This is too tough," "This is too old," he says of the others. At last he finds one that suits him. "This one will do," he says. The Buyer and the Market Woman take hold of the Chicken, one by each arm, and swing it three times. If the Chicken laughs, or if his arms give way while he is being swung, he is put out of the game.

The Buyer then goes to market again to buy and swing another Chicken. This goes on until all have been sold.

FOLLOW CHASE

14-30 players, 6-10 years   *Indoors or out of doors*

Players are chosen to be the Runner and the Chaser. The others stand in a circle, an arm's length apart. Each player puts out his arms and rests them on the shoulders of the players on each side of him. The intertwined arms make arches between the players. The Runner stands under an arch at one side of the circle and the Chaser under an arch opposite him. At a signal from the leader or a chosen player, the Runner begins to weave in and out of the arches around the circle. The Chaser follows after him, trying to follow in exactly the same path. If the Chaser catches the Runner, he becomes the Runner and another player takes the part of the Chaser. If the Chaser fails to follow the Runner exactly, he must exchange places with the player in the circle who first caught his mistake. The game goes on until all have had turns. If the running and chasing of two players go on too long, the leader may call "Time" and two others from the circle will take their places.

Norway

CUT THE OATS

7-21 players, 6-12 years   *Usually out of doors*

There should be an uneven number of players, who select one child to stand in the center of the circle. The others hold hands and skip around in a circle singing as they go:

Cut the oats to-geth-er.

Who shall help to bind them? It shall be my

own true love. Oh, tell me where to find him!

Yes-ter eve I saw him clear, The

moon-light on him shin-ing. Oh, you take yours and

I'll take mine! We'll leave the lone one pin-ing.

As the players sing, "You take yours and I'll take mine,"
the circle breaks up and partners are chosen. The one in the
center tries his best to get a partner. When all partners have
been chosen, one player will be left alone. That one must
stand in the center for the next playing of the game.

Portugal

THE GAME OF THE STONE
(Jogo da Pedra)

Out of doors   *Similar to Ninepins*

2-15 players, 10-14 years

The players find for themselves nine flat stones and nine round stones, each about as large as an apple. They place the round stones on the flat stones in a row. Each player in turn takes nine small stones, each one large enough to fit in the palm. He stands about fifteen feet from the nine stones and begins to throw at them. He scores one point for each round stone that he knocks off its flat stone base. When he has thrown his nine stones, he counts up his score and sets the round stones back on their bases. The next player throws and so on until all have had a turn. The player who has counted the highest score wins.

Russia

GORELKI

11-41 players, boys and girls, 8 years up to adults   *Out of doors*

There must be an unequal number of players. One is chosen to be It and the others divide into pairs, who line up, one behind the other. It stands at the head of the line. He calls, "Last pair run." The couple at the end of the line separate. One of them runs up each side of the line. They try to form a couple a few feet in front of It before he can catch either of them. If they succeed, It takes his place ahead of them and calls for another pair to run. If It catches one of the pair, he and the captured one form a couple at the head of the line.

The player who was not caught becomes the next It, who stands at the head of the line and calls for others to run. —*Seraphima Popovitsky Alexander, Russia.*

Russia: Ukraine

THE BEAR
(Medvid)

8-30 players, boys and girls, 7-12 years   *Out of doors*

A square field is marked off, large enough to accommodate the players without too much crowding. Inside the square an oblong space is marked off (by drawing on the ground with a stick, or placing lines of stones) to represent the Bear's den. One of the children is chosen to be the Big Bear or *Medvidisko* (meedvedeesko). When over twenty are playing, more than one Big Bear is chosen and several groups take part.

The Bear goes into his den and the players move about the field. Suddenly the Bear shouts from his den, "The Bear is coming!" He runs out of his den with his hands held together. He tries to catch a player by touching him with his locked hands. As soon as he has caught one, that player becomes a Bear and both run into the den.

They join hands and one of them announces, "The Bears are coming!" and they go hunting in the field. They are allowed to catch only one player at a time by touching him with their free hands. They must always keep together and not break apart. When the Big Bear and the Bear have succeeded in catching a third Bear, all three run into the den, join hands, and advance again. The Big Bear always stays at the end of the line, which grows in length until all the players have become Bears. Any player who goes into the den or steps out of the field becomes a Bear. The last player to be caught becomes the Big Bear for the next game.—*Mrs. Lubow Hansen, Kiev, Russia, and Washington, D. C.*

GRANDFATHER PANAS
(Did Panas)

Indoors or out of doors   *Similar to Blindman's Buff*
6-20 players, boys and girls, 6-10 years

One player is chosen to be It and he is blindfolded. The others stand around him and the following conversation takes place:

CHILDREN: What do you stand upon?

IT: Upon pins.

CHILDREN: How is it that they do not hurt you?

IT: I am wearing red boots.

CHILDREN: Who sewed them for you?

IT: Grandfather Panas.

CHILDREN: Then turn around and catch us.

It tries to catch one of the children. The one whom he catches becomes It for the next game.—*Mrs. Lubow Hansen, Kiev, Russia, and Washington, D. C.*

THE GYPSY
(Tyshan)

6-20 players, boys and girls, 6-12 years   *Indoors or out of doors*

The children choose one of their number to be the Gypsy. He sits down, surrounded by the other children, who are holding hands and moving slowly in a circle. Those in the circle chant or relate very slowly the following words, while the Gypsy acts out all that is told about him: "The first hour the Gypsy is asleep, the second hour the Gypsy is asleep, the third hour the Gypsy is asleep," and so on until the seventh hour has been mentioned. Then the chant changes: "The eighth hour the Gypsy gets up, the ninth hour the Gypsy dresses, the tenth hour the Gypsy washes, the eleventh hour the Gypsy gets ready, the twelfth hour—the Gypsy runs." At the last three words the children loosen their hands and run in all directions while the Gypsy chases them.

The one whom the Gypsy first catches becomes the next Gypsy.—*Mrs. Lubow Hansen, Kiev, Russia, and Washington, D. C.*

Scotland

KICK THE CAN

6-20 players, boys and girls, 8-14 years   *Out of doors*

The game is played with an empty tin can, in which stones or small articles that will rattle have been placed. One player is chosen to be It. A spot is chosen for goal, say a tree or a circle drawn on the ground. A player kicks the can away from the goal, making it go as far as possible. It runs after it, while the others hide. Before the game, the bounds for the hiding have been strictly set.

It brings the can back to the goal and sets it there. Then he seeks for the others. When he sees one, he runs back to the goal, picks up the can, shakes it, and calls, "One, two, three, I see (Tom)." If he succeeds in this, Tom is considered caught and It looks for other players. A player who has been seen may run and try to get to the goal before It does. If he succeeds, he kicks the can away from the goal. It must go after it as before and all those who have already been caught may run and hide again. If It sees three players, he must call out, "One, two, three, I see ——" for each one. Should It

succeed in catching all the players without the can being kicked from the goal, the last one caught becomes the next It.
—*Andrew Burt, Dunfermline, Scotland, and Halifax, Canada.*

THE SPANISH KNIGHT

10-20 players, usually girls, 8-10 years   *Indoors or out of doors*

One player is chosen to be the Spanish Knight. Others take the parts of the Mother, the Older Daughter, the Younger Daughter Jane, and the Attendants. The Knight comes up and sings to the Mother, Daughters, and Attendants:

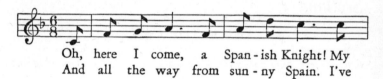

Oh, here I come, a Span-ish Knight! My
And all the way from sun-ny Spain. I've

sword is sharp, my spurs are bright.
come to court your daugh-ter Jane.

The Knight kneels before Jane and the Mother rejects him, saying:

> My daughter Jane is much too young;
> She cannot speak the Spanish tongue.

The Knight sings:

> So I'll away and I'll away,
> And I'll come back some other day.

The Older Daughter and Attendants sing:

> Come back, come back, your courting's free,
> And pick the fairest one you see.

The Knight chooses one of the group as he sings:
> The fairest one that I do see
> Is bonnie (Mary). Will you come with me?

The chosen one sings:
> I'll go with you, all robed in white.
> Tonight shall be our wedding night.

The two march out as the others sing:
> So they'll away and they'll away,
> But they'll come back some other day.

—*Andrew Burt, Dunfermline, Scotland, and Halifax, Canada.*

BAR THE DOOR

Out of doors   *Similar to Tag*
6-30 players, boys and girls, 8-14 years

In the town the game is played on the streets from one sidewalk to the other. About a hundred and fifty feet of the street mark the bounds of the playing ground. In the country or on a playground, the bounds are marked out, with a wide space in the middle and home goals at each end. The wide space should be about the width of a city street and the goals the width of a good-sized sidewalk.

One player is chosen to be It. The others line up on one side of the street. It calls one player by name and that player must cross to the other side while It chases him. The player may run along the pavement before starting across. It may not step on the pavement. If the player is caught, he joins It in trying to catch the others. But if the player reaches the other goal safely, he shouts, "Bar the door!" At this call, all the players must run across the street while It tries to tig (tag) and catch them. All those who are tagged must join It in catching the others.

The first player caught calls the name of one who is to run to the other goal. If he makes it safely, he calls, "Bar the door!" and all run. If the last man left uncaught can run from goal to goal three times without being tagged, he may call one player back to his side. This player calls another and so on until only one remains, who is It for next game. Otherwise the last man to be caught is It for the next game.—*Andrew Burt, Dunfermline, Scotland, and Halifax, Canada.*

Spain

MOON AND MORNING STARS

Out of doors   *Similar to Tag*
             5-25 players, 5-8 years

This is a game that comes from a warm land where there is bright sunshine and where trees and houses cast dark shadows on the ground. The children have made a game to play in the shadowy and sunny places. One player is chosen to be the Moon and she stands in the shadow of a house or large tree, because the moon belongs to the dark and must not go into the sunshine. The other players are Morning Stars and they dance around in the sunshine because they belong to the light. Sometimes they venture into the shadow where the Moon tries to tag them. As they dance in the sunshine, they sing a verse. The tune of "The Muffin Man" may be used:

> The bright Moon and the Morning Stars.
> The bright Moon and the Morning Stars.
> Where the light shines gay, we dance and play,
> But who will dare the shadow?

When the Moon succeeds in tagging a Star, that child becomes the next Moon.

Sweden

BOW AND CURTSY TAG

10-30 players, 6-10 years   *Indoors or out of doors*

The players form a circle, standing with their hands joined. One child is chosen to be It. He runs once or twice around the outside of the circle, finally touching one of the players on the shoulder. That player must run around the outside of the circle in the direction opposite to It. When the two meet, they must stop and greet each other. A player who is a boy must bow three times. A girl must curtsy three times. The greeting over, the two complete the rest of the circuit, still going in opposite directions. Each tries to reach the vacant place first. The one left without a place becomes It for the next game.

NUMBER GAME

Indoors or out of doors   *Similar to Tag*
6-20 players

The players scatter across the playing field and each one draws a circle around himself at about arm's length, either with a stick on the ground or with chalk on the floor. Each player stands within the circle he has drawn. One child, previously chosen to be It, gives a different number to each child who stands in a circle.

It calls out two of the numbers he has given. The players with those two numbers must change circles. It tries to get to one of the circles first. If he fails, he must call out two other numbers. If he succeeds, the player left without a circle becomes It for the next game.

Switzerland

EAGLE AND GOATS

7-15 players, boys and girls, 6-10 years   *Indoors or out of doors*

One player is chosen to be the Eagle and the others are Goats. The Goats pretend to be grazing in the pasture when the Eagle appears, swooping along with outspread arms, as if to catch them in his claws. The Goats have to guess quickly which one the Eagle plans to attack and quickly hide him in a circle. If they guess right, the Eagle flies away and they pretend to graze again. If they guess wrong, the Eagle calls aloud the name of the one he seeks. Unless that one is quickly circled, the Eagle catches him and drags him off. The game continues until all the Goats but one have been caught. That one becomes the Eagle for the next game.

THE GOATHERD

6-15 players, 8-10 years   *Out of doors*

One player is chosen to be the Goatherd. He chooses some stones to represent his Goats. He places them in a pile or scatters them close together. Then he lies down beside them and pretends to fall asleep. He has his horn beside him. (In this country a whistle could be used.) The other players surround him. One of them creeps up to the Goats and tries to run off with one of them before the Goatherd sees him and blows his horn. If the player succeeds, the Goatherd has lost a Goat. If the horn blows, the player is caught and must become the next Goatherd.

Index